LANGUAGE IN UGANDA

PETER LADEFOGED • RUTH GLICK • CLIVE CRIPER

LANGUAGE IN
ETHIOPIA
KENYA
TANZANIA
UGANDA
ZAMBIA

With an introduction by CLIFFORD H. PRATOR
and additional material by LIVINGSTONE WALUSIMBI

This study was partly subsidized by funds from the Ford Foundation who also financed the Survey of Language Use and Language Teaching in Eastern Africa. The present volume is co-sponsored by the Makerere Institute of Social Research.

LONDON • 1972
OXFORD UNIVERSITY PRESS
NEW YORK • NAIROBI • TORONTO

Oxford University Press, Ely House, London W. 1

GLASGOW NEW YORK TORONTO MELBOURNE WELLINGTON
CAPE TOWN IBADAN NAIROBI DAR ES SALAAM LUSAKA ADDIS ABABA
DELHI BOMBAY CALCUTTA MADRAS KARACHI LAHORE DACCA
KUALA LUMPUR SINGAPORE HONG KONG TOKYO

Oxford University Press, P.O. Box 72532, Nairobi.

Cover design by Amrik Singh

This book is for CLIFFORD PRATOR.
It is not the book he wanted
but it is the best that we could do.

Contents

Acknowledgements

This book would not have been possible without the help of many people, notably: Pio Zirimu, Mathias Mosha, Ali Mazrui, Lionel Billows, Carol Scotton, Donald Mann, Louise Pirouet and Dee Norton, all of Makerere University College; Charles Musisi, William Harrison and James Heaton of the Buloba Language Unit; James Aryada and Arthur Bagunywa of the Ministry of Education; Michael Nsimbi, Dorothy Galer, George Allen, Livingstone Walusimbi; Clifford Lutton, the Associate Director of the Survey; and the following Makerere students who assisted as fieldworkers: Pascal Aidu, Andrew Aliat, James Bagenda, Raphael Bitamizire, John Kalema, Peter Maniraguha, John Ogwana, Christopher Okot, John Otim, E. Rwivanga, Jesse Wasega-Mutenga and Albert Yobo.

The authors and publishers would also like to thank Dr J. Donald Bowen for his valuable editorial assistance.

Introduction

Clifford H. Prator

GENESIS OF THE SURVEY

The publication of *Language in Uganda* is the most tangible result yet achieved by the Survey of Language Use and Language Teaching in Eastern Africa. Officially begun in the summer of 1967 and scheduled to continue at least until mid-1971, the Survey is an attempt to respond to the need, expressed with increasing urgency in recent years by African political and educational leaders, for certain types of information about languages.

The Survey has been directed toward the achievement of four principal goals:

1. To gather and disseminate basic information on the use and teaching of languages in Ethiopia, Kenya, Tanzania, Uganda and Zambia.
2. To stimulate research and development in linguistics and language pedagogy in the region.
3. To assist in strengthening the resources of eastern African institutions concerned with the language arts and sciences.
4. To foster closer, productive, intraregional and international relations among specialists in linguistics and related disciplines.

The activities judged most likely to achieve these aims have included the provision of financial support for local research and development projects, grants to Africans for specialized training, the dissemination of publications and bibliographical information, support for the organization of national language associations, and the holding of the first Eastern African Regional Conference on Language and Linguistics in Dar es Salaam on 18–21 December 1968. A detailed account of these activities has been published in a quarterly *Bulletin.**

Conducted as an independent academic undertaking, the Survey could nonetheless have never hoped to operate without the full

*The *Bulletin* has been distributed without charge to interested readers by the Survey Office, P.O. Box 30641, Nairobi, Kenya.

knowledge and approval of the government of each of the five countries involved. The Government of Uganda was the first to be called on repeatedly for support, which it has given most generously in the form of permissions, relevant data, and the advice of appropriate officials. But *Language in Uganda* is even more directly and substantially indebted to Makerere University College, which has made available to the country-study team office space and equipment, given its members visiting faculty status, administered grant funds, and provided a stimulating and congenial setting for the work of writing. Above all, the encouragement and shared wisdom of Makerere faculty colleagues have been invaluable.

Final policy control of the Survey and the ultimate responsibility for carrying it out have been exercised by an academic council, meeting semi-annually with ministry officials as observers, composed of representatives of the national universities of the five participating countries. Haile Sellassie I University has been represented by Hailu Fulass, Assistant Professor of Ethiopian Languages, and Richard Pankhurst, Director of the Institute of Ethiopian Studies; The University College, Nairobi, by Thomas P. Gorman, Lecturer in English, and Bethwell A. Ogot, Dean of the Faculty of Arts; The University College, Dar es Salaam, by Mohammed Abdulaziz, Lecturer in Language and Linguistics, and Ralph J. Wingfield, Senior Lecturer in Education; Makerere University College by E. Lionel Billows, Head of the Department of Language Method, Ali Mazrui, Dean of the Faculty of Social Sciences, and Pio Zirimu, Lecturer in English (in rotation); and the University of Zambia by Dorothea Lehmann, Senior Research Fellow in the Centre for African Studies, and Krishna Rayan, Professor of English.

The basic concepts which gave rise to the Survey were elaborated over a period of several years by a rather large group of individuals including both Africans and non-Africans concerned with language in Africa. It is the extensiveness of the interested group that gives reason to hope that the Survey, with its severe limitations on manpower, will prove to be only one early episode in a continuing effort carried out along similar lines.

As far back as 1961, the specialists who gathered from all over the world—appropriately enough, at Makerere College in Uganda—for the Commonwealth Conference on the Teaching of English as a Second Language noted in their report that:

2

The organizers of this Conference had difficulty in obtaining the information needed to ensure that its members would be adequately informed about the uses of English, about the place of English in the educational system, and about experiment and research on all aspects of English as a second language. Statistical information from one country is not readily comparable with that from another. In most cases statistics about the use, as opposed to the teaching, of English are not collected.*

The representatives from African countries deplored the fact that, while not enough was known about the conditions under which English was used and taught, much less information was available about the social and educational function of the languages of Africa.

In 1962 the National Advisory Council on the Teaching of English as a Foreign Language, newly established to advise American Government agencies regarding their TEFL activities, recommended as one of the 'Decisions' reached at its May meeting that a study in depth of the language situation of a developing country in Africa be carried out in connection with an internationally sponsored English-speaking project. Similarly, the International Conference on Second Language Problems, a semi-official Anglo-Franco-American group which meets annually to review developments in the teaching of languages of wider communication, has long been convinced that the basic linguistic information necessary for mounting a truly effective programme of English or French instruction is simply not available in most African countries. Since its meeting in Nijmegen, Holland, in February 1962, the Conference has repeatedly called for research on a country basis, but with international staffing, of exactly the kind undertaken by the Survey.

To the impetus given by those involved in the teaching of English and French in Africa was added that provided by the rapidly increasing group primarily concerned with the analysis and teaching of African languages, within Africa and overseas. Significantly, the two groups envisaged no conflict of interests. One of the concepts basic to the Survey, then, has been the recognition that language can be regarded as a unitary human phenomenon and that, in the final analysis, any effort made to cast light on how one language is best handled in a given setting should help define the role of all languages in the same setting.

*Report of the Commonwealth Conference on the Teaching of English as a Second Language, Government Printer, Entebbe, 1961, p. 41.

3

An obvious forerunner of the present survey in Eastern Africa was the West African Languages Survey sponsored by the universities of that area and begun in 1960 under the direction of Joseph H. Greenberg with the financial backing of the Ford Foundation. This trail-blazing attempt to survey the language situation in an entire region has concentrated on the more narrowly linguistic problems of describing little known languages. The publications coming out of it are technical articles and monographs of more direct interest to professional linguists than to government officials or language teachers. As a by-product of this survey, however, the linguist investigators have accumulated a considerable store of information on the general language situation in West African countries, and Greenberg now plans to proceed with a complete revision of the Westermann and Bryan *Languages of West Africa*, which is the basic handbook of information now available to the general public.

In the fall of 1965 the Ford Representative for East and Central Africa, Francis X. Sutton, was impressed by the number of language projects being proposed within the region and by the great need, emphasized in the proposals, for basic information that could be applied to the solution of the pressing linguistic problems faced by each country. Since he had been one of the chief proponents of the West African Languages Survey, it naturally occurred to him that a similar programme might be called for in Eastern Africa. At his invitation, Charles A. Ferguson, then of the Center for Applied Linguistics in Washington, and Clifford H. Prator of the University of California, Los Angeles, visited Nairobi, Addis Ababa, Kampala, and Dar es Salaam early in 1966 in order to assess the situation. They were asked by the Foundation to try to answer two fundamental questions: (1) was the situation ripe and were there adequate resources for a language survey of Eastern Africa; and (2) if so, how should the work be planned so as to provide the types of information that would be of most practical value to administrators and educators?

Consultations with academicians and ministry officials in the countries visited led swiftly to the conclusion that the situation was indeed ripe, in the sense that the need for a survey was widely felt and strong local support would be forthcoming. On the other hand, the human resources necessary to carry out such a project on a regional scale were clearly not then available within the area.

4

While there were small groups of trained linguists in several of the capitals, they were fully committed—even over-committed—in strategic positions. To take them away from their jobs for full-time research would amount to hamstringing their departments and endangering what progress had been made toward developing institutional pools of linguistic expertise. Their ranks badly needed reinforcement, and most key personnel would have to be brought in from outside.

The answer to the second question was not so easily arrived at; the best that could be done was to offer certain hypotheses that would then be tested in the course of the survey. The most frequent linguistic questions with which the governments of Eastern Africa were faced involved a few major languages rather than the great number of minor tongues. Therefore the survey should concern itself primarily with such languages as Amharic, Swahili, and English. Policy decisions depended more often on the social role of languages than on their structural qualities, hence more attention should be paid to language use than to linguistic analysis. Since reliance must be placed chiefly on the schools for the implementation of language policy, the survey must provide information on the effectiveness of language teaching. Because choices must be made among the widely divergent forms in which most African languages are spoken, perhaps the techniques that the sociolinguists were developing for studying linguistic diversity would be relevant.

One of the most interesting current developments in linguistic studies and one which has had a considerable influence on the thinking that led to the survey is the emergence of sociolinguistics as a recognized area for interdisciplinary investigation. There is still disagreement as to the range of matters sociolinguists should concern themselves with, but one pioneer practitioner offers the following tentative definition of the term:

It is certainly correct to say that sociolinguistic studies . . . deal with the relationship between language and society. But such a statement is excessively vague. If we attempt to be more exact, we may note that sociolinguistics differs from some earlier interests in language-society relationships in that . . . it considers language as well as society to be a structure, rather than merely a collection of items. The sociolinguist's task is then to show the systematic covariance of linguistic structure and social structure—and perhaps even to show a causal relationship in one direction or the other. However, although sociolinguists derive much of their approach from structural linguistics, at the same time they break sharply with one linguistic trend. This is the approach which treated

5

languages as completely uniform, homogeneous or monolithic in their structure; in this view . . . differences in speech habits found within a community were swept under the rug as "free variation". One of the major tasks of sociolinguistics is to show that such variation or diversity is not in fact "free", but is correlated with systematic social differences. In this and in still larger ways, linguistic *diversity* is precisely the subject matter of sociolinguistics.*

This definition is quite restrictive, but in practice many socio-linguists have envisaged the possibility of applying their methods to the solution of the practical problems of the language planner, and have seen in the survey an opportunity to attempt such applications. Thus, an *ad hoc* Committee on Sociolinguistic Research in Africa, meeting at Palo Alto under the co-chairmanship of Joseph Greenberg and Jack Berry in January 1966, unanimously endorsed the notion of a sociolinguistically oriented language survey of Eastern Africa and spelt out in detail the kind of research they had in mind.

A formal proposal for the survey, prepared by Ferguson and Prator, was considered, revised, and elaborated by representatives of the national universities of Ethiopia, Kenya, Tanzania, Uganda and Zambia at a prototype Survey Council meeting held at Molo, Kenya, on 17–18 September 1966. In the spring of 1967 the rather complicated arrangements whereby the University of East Africa would administer the research funds, the University of California at Los Angeles would staff the Survey Office, and the Center for Applied Linguistics would provide an international Advisory Committee were worked out. The Advisory Committee was included in the plans so that the survey might benefit by the collaboration of leading non-African specialists in African languages, social science, and language teaching, and so as to insure the support of academic circles outside of Eastern Africa.†

---

*William Bright, *Sociolinguistics, Proceedings of the UCLA Sociolinguistics Conference, 1964*, Mouton, The Hague, 1966, p. 11. See also Alfred Pietrzyk *et al., Selected Titles in Sociolinguistics*, Center for Applied Linguistics, Washington, 1964 (with supplements).
†The membership of the Advisory Committee has been: J. Donald Bowen, Professor of English, University of California, Los Angeles (*ex officio*); Charles A. Ferguson, Chairman of the Committee on Linguistics, Stanford University (Chairman); Joshua A. Fishman, Dean of the Ferkauf Graduate School of Education, Yeshiva University; Wallace E. Lambert, Professor of Psychology, McGill University; T. F. Mitchell, Professor of Modern English, Leeds University; Eugene Nida, The American Bible Society; Edgar Polomé, Professor of Linguistics, University of Texas; Clifford H. Prator, Vice-Chairman, Department of English, University of California, Los Angeles (*ex officio*); A. Hood Roberts, Assistant Director, Center for Applied Linguistics (Vice-Chairman); Franklin P. Rolfe, Dean of the College of Letters and Science, University of California,

In the late spring the Ford Foundation approved the funds for an initial two-year period of operation, the recruitment of field personnel was intensified, and the participating universities in Eastern Africa appointed their official representatives to the Survey Council. With the arrival in Nairobi on 25 July 1967, of Clifford L. Lutton, Assistant to the Field Director, to set up the central office, the Survey of Language Use and Language Teaching in Eastern Africa could be said to be under way.

QUESTIONS THAT HAVE BEEN ASKED

The Survey hopes to produce a series of five country studies. It was agreed that the series would be written primarily for Africans who are professionally concerned with language problems. In order to make the studies accessible to relatively wide readership, technical terminology would be reduced to a minimum and an effort would be made to explain such concepts as might not be familiar to the non-specialist. The most complicated statistical tables would be relegated to appendices or to the monographs and articles intended for research scholars to which the Survey is also expected to give rise. Each country study will be prepared by an inter-disciplinary team of three scholars working in the country for a period of twelve to fifteen months, with such aid as local scholars can afford to give and the Survey Office can supply from Nairobi.

Those who have felt the need for the Survey are convinced that all the countries of Eastern Africa, as a matter of national development or even of continued national existence, must answer a set of language questions. The policy decisions which the answers constitute then require implementation, often on a large scale and over long periods of time.*

Some of these questions are of *language choice*. Which language(s) shall be the official language(s) of government, used in laws, administration, police work and the armed forces? Which shall be taught

Los Angeles; Earl Stevick, Foreign Service Institute; Peter Strevens, Chairman of the Department of Modern Languages, University of Essex; and Wilfred H. Whiteley, Professor of Bantu Languages, School of Oriental and African Studies, University of London.
*This 'Introduction' incorporates without further acknowledgement extensive quotations and paraphrases from the unpublished documents prepared in order to explain the Survey to ministries, universities, and the Foundation. Since several different people had a hand in writing the documents and they were revised by a number of committees, it is no longer possible to give credit exactly where credit is due.

7

as subjects and which used as the medium or media of instruction at the various levels of formal education? What language(s) must be accepted for use on the radio and television, in publishing, in telecommunications?

Associated with these questions are the basic problems of *language instruction*. What is the most efficient way of implementing language policy through the schools? What degree and type of proficiency is required in various tongues? Are available resources—in terms of schools, teachers, and instructional materials—adequate for each language? What are the difficulties in teaching a particular language to a particular group of people?

Other questions involve *'language engineering'*. Once a language has been chosen for certain purposes, it may be necessary to take steps to insure its adequacy for those purposes. The questions to be answered generally refer to standardization and modernization. How standard are existing 'standard' languages? What variety of each should be selected or created as the preferred form for use in writing and speaking? What means should be employed to provide new terminology and the needed scientific and literary forms of discourse?

Viable language policies will naturally be motivated by such often stated national social and political goals as: (1) unity, to be achieved through the elimination of divisions based on race, tribe, religion and economic status; (2) a clearer definition of the national cultural identity; (3) an improved standard of living for the individual citizen; (4) greater access to knowledge, especially in the fields of science and technology; and (5) Pan-Africanism tempered by relationships with both East and West.

It is also obvious that language policies, like many other national policies, are not in practice determined solely by rational considerations and logic. Indeed decisions on language questions are notoriously influenced by emotional issues such as tribal identifications, religious loyalties, national rivalries, racial prejudices, the desire to preserve élites, and so on. They may even run directly counter to all the evidence of feasibility, as did Somalia's attempt to make Arabic the official language despite the fact that almost the entire population speaks Somali and knows relatively little Arabic.

All the scholars connected with the Survey are well aware that nearly all these questions are political issues which must be decided by the appropriate people. But as academicians and rationalists,

8

scholars must believe that the answers worked out to language questions will be useful only to the extent that they square with linguistic and social facts. Policies will be efficacious only in so far as they succeed in reconciling national goals with actual possibilities. And if choices are made on emotional grounds alone, they cannot be expected to prove maximally productive. It is even desirable for the policy maker to have at his disposal as many facts as possible about the strength and nature of the emotional issues.

Since policy making is an endless process, the need for more and better information can never be entirely satisfied. No country can be said to have a definitive and fully implemented language policy— not Ethiopia nor Tanzania, not even long-existing countries like Russia and France, and certainly not Uganda. A major policy decision such as that to make Swahili the national language of Tanzania leads inevitably to the need for subsidiary decisions: up to what grade level should Swahili be used as the sole medium of instruction in the schools; should an effort be made to preserve the tribal languages; what is to be the eventual role of English? Each of these questions leads in turn to a further set of questions, and the process is repeated indefinitely as the fabric of policy is woven. Meanwhile there are changes in the political regime, shifts in international relations, internal and external economic developments, and new cultural interests, all of which cause established policies to be regarded in a new light. There are successes as well as failures in the implementation of policy, from both of which lessons can be learned. The day comes when major decisions made in the past are modified or reversed, and a large segment of the fabric has to be rewoven. It would thus seem that the range of information needed by those who formulate and implement language policy is very broad, that very detailed information is needed at certain stages, and that the need is permanent.

The planners of the Survey recognized that each of the country studies must differ somewhat from all the others. First of all, there would be divergences reflecting the fact that the five countries are at very different stages in their development of language policies. Tanzania has recently opted for a vigorous pro-Swahili policy, which makes it advisable that the country study concentrate much of its attention on Swahili and on facts relevant to policy implementation. The pro-Amharic policy of Ethiopia has been in effect longer, and the pressures for some recognition of other languages such as Tigrigna are perhaps stronger there. In Zambia, English seems to be very firmly entrenched and there is no very likely indigenous candidate for the role of national language; what is most needed is information on the teaching of English as well as on the possibilities of developing Chibemba and Chinyanja as 'union' languages. Kenya is simultaneously backing the introduction of English at earlier age levels, favouring more use of Swahili in the mass media, and considering the idea of a return to vernacular instruction. Policy makers in Uganda appear to be torn in even more different directions. Almost no element of language policy can be regarded as fixed beyond challenge, and long-term plans for implementation must await basic decisions.

There would also be divergences arising from the fact that the types and amounts of information available vary from country to country. There is notably less known about the Sudanic, Nilotic, and Cushitic languages to the north than about the Bantu languages to the south. Much more research is needed into the linguistic geography of Ethiopia than into that of Zambia, where relatively refined language maps exist for many areas.

More facts about the teaching of African languages appear to be available in Tanzania than in Kenya or Uganda. The size of the national stocks of information of different types is naturally related to the existence of specialized agencies in certain countries: the University Testing Centre in Ethiopia, the Buloba Language Unit in Uganda, the Curriculum Development and Research Centre in Kenya, the Institute for Swahili Research in Tanzania, and the Zambia Language Survey in Zambia.

There would be still another type of divergences, those related to the human factors in the undertaking. Though an effort would be made to achieve an interdisciplinary balance in the composition of the teams, the areas of scholarly competence represented were sure to vary widely from team to team. A team led by a linguist with a background in experimental phonetics neither could nor should be expected to work in a way exactly similar to the way in which a team headed by a specialist in language teaching would work. Since no one could be sure in advance just how an experimental venture like the Survey should be carried out, it was desirable to encourage a certain amount of methodological variation.

If it is clear that each of the five studies must be expected to provide somewhat different kinds of information, it is nonetheless

10

true that some types of fact are almost universally needed and that information that would be comparable from country to country is of particular value. In order to achieve as high a degree as possible of comparability in the series, the Survey's planners suggested that all of the studies should include data relevant to at least three major areas of concern. These may be identified as *language and society, language in education* and *language teaching.* The teams would seek to enumerate the languages used in each country, to determine who speaks which languages where and for what purposes, to discover what factors contribute to the choice of one language instead of another, and to find out what attitudes are held by the various segments of the society toward the several languages used. The studies would also include information regarding the extent to which the facilities for learning languages provided by the schools and other agencies are meeting the linguistic needs of the society; the levels of attainment, in terms of concept formation and specific language skills, among children entering and leaving the educational system; the main problems of regression; the levels of language performance among teachers. Similarly, the teams would investigate the appropriateness of the methods employed in language instruction, the provision made for the development of teaching materials, the adequacy of teacher training, and the major sources of interference by the first language in the learning of subsequent languages.

In all five studies the emphasis would be placed on factual data rather than on the author's opinions, in so far as it is possible to separate the two. Opinions insufficiently supported by facts, often presented as if they were facts, have long beclouded many of the issues involved. The Survey is basically an attempt to provide more facts. This attention to factual information would be all the more advisable since most of the authors would not be Africans; it is presumably easier for a non-African to err in an opinion about Africa than in a fact about Africa. It would seem especially unwise for the authors to cast themselves in the role of policy makers, to take sides on top priority issues such as the choice of a national language. These are political questions which call for authoritative local decisions.

On the other hand, it would be futile to pretend that opinions have nothing to do with the way in which facts are gathered and evaluated, or that a scholar—particularly one working in the social sciences or the applied humanities (e.g. language teaching)—can always be quite certain that the results of his research are indeed facts rather than disguised opinions. Even if all expression of the authors' opinions could be eliminated from the country studies, it is doubtful that this would be desirable. There are many technical questions on which a research scholar has a better right to have an opinion than does the average layman. The elimination of all indications of opinion from the studies would tend to sterilize them and to minimize their impact and relevance to practical concerns. It would also tend to disappoint the hopes of educators and administrators in Africa who have been looking to the Survey for effective aid in dealing with some of the problems with which they are faced from day to day.

As is always the case in an apparent dilemma of this sort, the solution would seem to lie in the exercise of careful discrimination. The emphasis on factual data must be maintained. The authors should not hesitate, however, to raise questions of opinion which they themselves have no intention of trying to answer but which seem to have been overlooked. They should feel free in many cases to point out the possible relevance of facts to much discussed questions of opinion. They should even be allowed an occasional expression of their own opinions in matters they judge to fall within their area of technical competence, provided that they make every effort never to present opinion as fact and that they resolutely leave policy making to the people of the country.

If what has been said on the preceding pages about the entire series of country studies is rethought in terms of Uganda, the questions that have been asked can be presented in much more specific form.

Questions regarding *language and society* could be stated in the following way:

What is the best way of carrying out a survey of language use and language teaching on a national scale?

Does the present system of education, with its great reliance on English, tend to produce progressively more marked stratification in Ugandan society? What vocational possibilities does a knowledge of English open up to a child? To what extent is mastery of English connected with economic advancement?

To what kinds and amounts of reading material would an education conducted entirely in Luganda give access at present?

12

How widely is Swahili used in comparison with English and Luganda? Is the antipathy to Swahili that was formerly prevalent in some parts of Uganda beginning to disappear?

Through which language is the Asian element in the population most likely to achieve integration? How many languages should be recognized in a census of Uganda? What is the relation between what people claim about their own linguistic ability and the language abilities they in fact have?

Which of the vernacular languages are the most similar? Is it possible to measure the degree of intelligibility between two languages? If radio broadcasts in Dhopadhola were eliminated, for example, could the Jopadhola be expected to understand broadcasts in Lango? What factors affect the success of such a change in language policy?

Among the significant questions regarding *language in education* are the following:

Under what circumstances are the language policies laid down by the Ministry of Education not observed in practice? How do language teachers regard the help given them by inspectors?

At what point do pupils now attain permanent literacy in English? What success is the Ministry having in its efforts to begin the use of English as the medium of instruction at an earlier level?

Is secondary school the best level at which to introduce the study of Swahili?

In what non-Baganda districts can a teacher who speaks only Luganda be expected to function effectively? What is the effect of using Luganda, a Bantu language, as the initial medium of instruction in the Sebei district, where the principal vernacular is non-Bantu?

Is there justification for adult literacy work in languages that are never taught in the schools? Why should a widely spoken language like Runyarwanda not be approved by the Ministry of Education for school use? How can the AID sponsored regional teacher training college that is to be developed at Gulu provide for the needs of teachers who will be giving instruction in both Sudanic and Nilotic languages?

13

What are the language needs of special groups such as diplomats, and how can they best be met?

Pertinent queries regarding *language teaching* include:

Does instruction through the medium of a second language contribute to the pupils' tendency to parrot words rather than to formulate ideas? If so, how can the tendency be countered? Are visual aids adequate, and who should supply them? What opportunities are given pupils to hear English spoken by people whose mother tongue is English?

How can English instruction best contribute to the country's educational and social goals? What reading materials in English, but with local subject matter, are available? How should teaching literature in a second language differ from teaching literature in the mother tongue?

How good are the present textbooks for teaching English in the elementary grades? Is there justification for abandoning the present incomplete series of textbooks and beginning the preparation of an entirely new series? In what way could the Buloba Language Unit most effectively work to strengthen language instruction?

Why do pupils in the Kigezi district often make the highest marks in English examinations?

How can vernacular instruction make a greater contribution to the Africanization of the curriculum? How can methods of teaching reading in the vernaculars and in English be more closely coordinated?

In what respects would it be easier for various groups such as the Baganda, Lango, and Lugbara to learn Swahili than to learn English?

Lest this imposing list of questions give a grossly exaggerated idea of what *Language in Uganda* was expected to accomplish, it is essential again to indicate that answers to most of them were simply not attempted. There is hardly a question on the list which, even if taken singly, could be answered definitively and in a fully documented form by the most diligent of scholars within the limitations of time imposed by the Survey. It would be impossible even to

14

estimate the total number of man-years of research that would be required to provide wholly satisfactory answers to the entire lot.

But research always proceeds by successive approximations to its goals. Limited as it had to be, the Survey has still brought to bear on the search for answers to this particular set of questions a significant amount of new manpower. The limitations have meant that, where there was insufficient opportunity to gather new objective evidence, recourse was had to seeking the help of the best qualified local observers. It was often necessary to use techniques designed to achieve rough results quickly rather than the very time-consuming and costly techniques that would have provided more accurate information about much more restricted areas of concern.

It is by the frequency with which it provides material for answers that the volume must be judged—and by the extent to which it makes possible the formulation of more and better questions.

15

The Ugandan Language Situation

This book presents an account of language in Uganda. The first part is an introductory section, giving an overview of the situation in the country as a whole, the historical background to this situation, and some data concerning the possibilities for different national languages. The second part describes the languages and their relationships to one another in more detail. The third part deals with the language factor in the educational system. The second and third parts are designed to be independent of one another, so that either can be read immediately after this introductory section. We had intended to include in this volume an additional part, giving data on the ways in which languages are actually used in Uganda. We have gathered a very large amount of information about the behaviour of both individuals and institutions with regard to language. Unfortunately the illness of one of the authors has resulted in our being able to present only a small fraction of this information in this introductory section. We hope to publish a second volume with more of our findings in the future.

Our general task was to discover the pattern of communication within Uganda. Usually it is easy to see how a nation communicates within itself. As long as all the people can speak, read, and write the same language, information can flow freely in all directions— from the government to the people, throughout religious, social and economic institutions such as churches, political parties, and nation-wide businesses, and among the people themselves. But in a country such as Uganda communications are not so simple. The nine million people are divided by more than 30 languages, so that the average person knows about events outside his own group only through a foreign language. In a country such as this there are numerous language problems.

The complexity of the present situation in Uganda is summarized in Map 1 (the foldout map at the end of the book) and Table 1.1 which contains data from the 1959 census and other official sources. As may be seen from the table, there are four major groups of

Ugandan languages: Bantu, Sudanic, Eastern Nilotic and Western Nilotic. The first three of these are as different as, say, English, Chinese, and Arabic; and even the Eastern and Western Nilotic groups differ from each other as much as English and French. It just so happens that Uganda is situated in the middle of Africa straddling the geographical limits reached by these very different groups of people.

Nearly two thirds of the people live in the southern part of Uganda and are members of the Bantu group. The 1959 census reported data on 15 tribes within this group, the largest single tribe being the Baganda,* who constitute a little more than 16 per cent of the population of the country as a whole. But statements concerning the number of tribes and their relative size may convey a misleading impression of the degree of linguistic diversity. Some of the languages of these different tribes are very similar to one another. If, for example, the political divisions could be disregarded, Luganda and Lusoga might just be considered to be very different dialects of the same language. This linguistic group would then constitute about 24 per cent of the country. Some of the Western Bantu languages are even more similar to one another than Luganda and Lusoga. Runyankore and Rukiga would be regarded by many people as dialects of the same language, as would Runyoro and Rutooro. It is even possible to regard all these four languages as a single unit totalling over 21 per cent of the country as a whole. The remaining Bantu languages, however, are all fairly different both from the two main groups and from each other.

The geographical distribution of the other major language groups in Uganda is considerably more complex. Successive waves of invaders have left a confused pattern of settlement with no clear cut boundaries between one ethnic group and another. In general it is possible to associate the North-East with the Eastern Nilotic group. The Iteso (the speakers of Ateso) are the largest single tribe in this group. The next largest (according to the 1959 census figures which were used in compiling Table 1.1) are the Karamojong. As we shall see in the next section, there are several subdivisions of this tribe and it is not at all clear whether it is really correct to speak of them as one tribe with one language.

*Readers who are unfamiliar with Bantu languages should note that these languages use systematic alternations of prefixes. The Baganda are the people who speak Luganda; they live in Buganda; and a single member of the tribe is a Muganda.

17

The extreme North-West of the country may be associated with the Sudanic languages, Lugbara and Madi. There are several forms of each of these languages. The central part of the North of Uganda is dominated by the Western Nilotic languages. The three largest, Lango, Acholi and Alur, are often considered to be variants of a single language called Lwo (not to be confused with the related Kenyan language Luo). Taken together, Lwo speakers amount to 12 per cent of the country.

There are several exceptions to these generalizations about the locations of the different groups of languages. Thus in the North-West, Kakwa, an Eastern Nilotic language, is spoken in what is predominantly a Sudanic area. Similarly in the East, groups of Western Nilotic Dhopadhola speakers and Eastern Nilotic Ateso speakers are interspersed within the Bantu speaking group.

Table 1.1 shows that there is no single language which is spoken as a first language by more than 16 per cent of the population. Even if we combine some of the languages listed in Table 1.1, we find that there is no linguistic group encompassing more than a quarter of the country. There are two linguistic groups (Luganda/ Lusoga; and Runyankore/Rukiga/Rutooro/Runyoro) which are respectively the first languages of only 24 and 20 per cent of the people of the country; two others (Lango/Acholi/Alur; and Ateso) which are the first languages of 12 and 8 per cent of the people respectively; and 14 other distinct languages each spoken by less than 6 per cent of the country. In addition there are at least 12 other distinct languages not listed in Table 1.1 which are each spoken by small groups of people which were not separately enumerated in the census.

We must also note the status of three other languages used in Uganda. The first of these, English, is not spoken as a mother tongue by any measurable percentage of Ugandan residents. But the Indian languages, Gujerati and Hindi, are spoken by a sizeable number of people who migrated to Uganda during the early part of the twentieth century.

The remaining columns in Table 1.1 show the effect of the linguistic situation on the policy of government agencies and commercial interests. For several government agencies there is a conflict between the desire to communicate effectively with all parts of the country, and the need to economize in resources and build national unity. There are many aspects of this dilemma, but since nearly all of them

TABLE 1.1: The status of the major languages spoken in Uganda.

	% population native speakers	hours/week radio	% non-English radio time	Newspapers: % of total circulation	Literacy campaign	Officially used in primary schools	Agriculture Information services	Law courts
BANTU								
(Eastern Ugandan)								
Luganda	16.3	34	29	40	X	X	X	
Lusoga	7.8	6¼	5		X			
Lumasaba (Lugisu)	5.1	4½	4					
Lugwere	1.7	—	0					
Lunyole	1.4	—	0					
Lusamia/Lugwe	1.3	3½	3		X			
Group totals	33.6	48¼	41	40				
(Western Ugandan)								
Runyankore	8.1	⎫ 9¾	⎫ 8	⎫ 0.8	X	X		
Rukiga	7.1	⎭	⎭	⎭	X	⎫ X		
Rutooro/Runyoro	6.2	9¼	8	0.8	X	⎭ X	X	
Runyarwanda	5.9	—	0					
Rurundi	2.0	—	0		X			
Rukonjo	1.7	—	0		X			
Rwamba	0.5	—						
Group totals	30.5	19	16	1.6				
WESTERN NILOTIC								
Lango	5.6	12¾	⎫ 11	2.1	X	⎫ X	X	
Acholi	4.4	3¼	⎭ 3		X	⎭		
Alur	1.9	½	0.5	0.2	X	X		
Dhopadhola	1.6	½	0.5		X			
Kumam	1.0							
Group totals	14.5	17	15	2.3				

TABLE 1.1: The status of the major languages spoken in Uganda (cont.)

	% population native speakers	hours/week radio	% non-English radio time	Newspapers: % of total circulation	Literacy campaign	Officially used in primary schools	Agriculture Information services	Law courts
EASTERN NILOTIC								
Ateso	8.3	12¾	11	0.9	X	X	X	
Ngakarimojong	2.0	3¼	3		X			
Kakwa	0.6	¾	0.5		X			
Kupsabiny (Sebei)	0.6	3	3					
Group totals	11.3	19¾	17.5	0.9				
CENTRAL SUDANIC								
Lugbara	3.7	5¼	4	0.2	X	X		
Madi	1.2	3½	3	0.1	X			
Group totals	4.9	8¾	7	0.3				
NON-UGANDAN								
Swahili	—	—	0	2.4		(X)		
English	0.2	50¾	—	50.5		X	X	X
Gujerati	1.0	—	0	2.0				
Hindustani (Hindi/Urdu)	0.1	5	4					

20

involve political considerations it would be improper for us to do more than to state the problem and present the data we have available. The underlying basic issue is the extent to which the present social and cultural needs of the individual speaker of a particular language have to be sacrificed in the interests of the present and future political and economic development of the country as a whole. Obviously it would be most convenient for the individual if he could read, write, and conduct all his affairs in his own language; but it is apparent that it is not in the national interest administratively and economically for a country to be split into so many small units.

Different agencies of the Government appear to have different answers to this problem. Thus Table 1.1 shows that Radio Uganda put out programmes in 16 Uganda languages as well as English and Hindustani. The number of hours per week for each language shown in Table 1.1 is that occurring in September 1968. In some cases it was difficult to decide in which language a programme was being broadcast; Radio Uganda often does not distinguish between some of the Western languages, and even puts on discussion programmes in which speakers of Runyankore, Rukiga, Rutooro and Runyoro talk to one another each using his own language. It should also be noted that the times listed in Table 1.1 may give an inflated impression of the amount of broadcasting in each language. Many of the programmes consist of recorded music presented under a title such as 'Lumasaba Requests'.

The discrepancies between the percentage of the country speaking a language and the percentage of the radio time devoted to that language may also be misleading. The figures given in Table 1.1 refer to the number of people speaking each language as a first language. As we shall see later, a larger number of people speak some of these languages as second languages.

The Ministry of Community Development, which is responsible for literacy campaigns, follows a similar policy to that of Radio Uganda. There have been literacy campaigns in 20 different languages. There is, however, very little for people to read in many of them. Our figures for newspaper circulation show that there are regular publications in only 8 different Ugandan languages; and, apart from the booklets written for the literacy campaign, there have been very few books published in most of these languages.

The policy of the Ministry of Education is to use six Ugandan

21

languages in the primary schools, and English in the secondary schools and higher education. These six languages are spoken by 61 per cent of the population; but, as we shall see later, in practice only a little more than half the children who are in school are being taught in their own language. Since the official language of the army and the police is Swahili, the Ministry of Education allows Swahili to be used in the special schools for children of the police or the army. The practice and policy of the Ministry of Education are described in more detail in the last half of this book.

Since Uganda is primarily an agricultural country, with 95 per cent of the population living in rural areas, it is interesting to note the languages used by the Ministry of Agriculture Information Services. We understand that they limit themselves (primarily for economic reasons) to printing their leaflets giving advice to farmers in English and only four Ugandan languages. But it should also be remembered that Uganda is a country where information travels primarily by word of mouth. There is evidence* that many more farmers heard about such things as the agricultural subsidy scheme, or the use of fertilizers, directly from the local Ministry of Agriculture representatives rather than from information given out on the radio or in the newspapers.

Finally in this brief survey of the languages officially used in different circumstances we must note that in the law courts theoretically only English is used. We say theoretically because we found that this often did not happen in practice. As one clerk of the court said to us, when talking about the local magistrate: 'That man, he will tell you he uses English. But he is a Muganda and when we all understand Luganda why should he use English?' (But another local magistrate remarked to us: 'I find it convenient to have everything translated into English for me, even when I know the local language. It gives me more time to think about my questions and their answers.')

THE HISTORICAL BACKGROUND

In order to understand the language situation in Uganda, we must consider the historical background. The position of English goes back to the fact that in 1894 the British Government took

*From the research of Mr. J. B. Walimbwa of the Ministry of Agriculture Information and Visual Aids Centre.

22

over rule of the area from the chartered East African Company and proclaimed a British Protectorate. The special status of Luganda ultimately has its roots in an agreement which was signed with the Kingdom of Buganda in 1900, in which special status was accorded to Baganda practices and political institutions, thus setting them apart from the three kingdoms in the West and all the other administrative areas in the East and North of the Protectorate. Initially all contact of the Europeans was with the Baganda and to a lesser (and more hostile) extent with the other kingdoms. The economic and educational advantages of this contact were largely the monopoly of the Baganda. In the early part of the century they were used as colonial agents to establish a hierarchy of chiefs and bureaucracy similar to their own in the Nilotic and Sudanic areas to the North and in the non-centralized Bantu areas of the East. This hierarchy of administrative units paralleling the Baganda system continues today.

The power and influence of the Baganda under the patronage of the British ensured the high status of their language and its position as a language of administration. Though the influence of Luganda in the Nilotic and Sudanic areas of the North has not lasted after the replacement of the Baganda agents by locally appointed chiefs, in certain districts of the East, e.g. Busoga, Bugisu, it has remained the official language taught in schools and used for public notices, and meetings. Nevertheless even among speakers of the closely related Bantu languages of Lusoga and Lumasaba it has remained an alien language whose use and practice has depended upon the continuing high status, power and achievement of the Baganda themselves.

When independence was achieved in 1962, the Kingdom of Buganda was granted federal status with exclusive powers over its public services as well as powers over hereditary and ceremonial offices and other customary matters. Only the latter powers were given to the other Kingdoms of Toro, Ankole and Bunyoro, and to Busoga. The remainder of the country was divided into a number of District Administrations. In 1967 the Kabaka (King) of Buganda was formally deposed and the federal and quasi-federal status of the kingdoms abolished. Though many Baganda remain in high positions in the civil service and elsewhere, this action has hastened the decline in their political power and prestige.

There has never been any substantial number of Europeans

23

c

living and working in Uganda. In 1966 there were estimated to be only 110,000 non-Africans of whom approximately 8 per cent were European and 80 per cent Asian. In 1948 only about a third of these numbers were present. Non-Africans have never been allowed to own land in Uganda, as they have been in Kenya. Consequently a situation has never existed in which there has been a European settler population; and the advent of comparatively large numbers of Asians is a recent phenomenon. Europeans have primarily been employed in missionary work, in administration, and in the provision of services, while the Asian population has been restricted to commercial activity within the towns and trading centres.

English was introduced as the major language of administration and law at the end of the nineteenth century. It is certainly now the dominant language among the leaders of the country. Swahili held a rival position for a short time in the first quarter of this century. It was not only used in the army and the police (as it still is), but was also taught in schools. The pro-Swahili policy, however, did not last for long. The Baganda viewed the introduction of Swahili both as a direct threat to their political power, and as a sign that Uganda might become like Kenya, dominated by a white settler population. Through the influence of the Baganda, English remained the official language. But, as we shall note in the next section, both Swahili and English now have important roles in the country as a whole.

NATIONAL LANGUAGES IN UGANDA

The first part of this introductory chapter gave data on the official use of languages in Uganda. We must now consider the extent to which any of these languages are national languages in the sense that they can or could figure predominantly as means of mass communication within Uganda. As part of the research on language use to be reported in detail later, we tried to estimate the current status of English, Luganda and Swahili. More than 2,000 people from all over the country were interviewed, and asked questions concerning their linguistic behaviour. We also conducted a number of reliability studies, in which we measured how accurately people answered our questions. The figures to be reported below take into account these reliability studies; and they have to some extent taken into account the fact that our sample was not properly

24

balanced for such factors as age, sex, and tribe in each district of Uganda. But they should nevertheless be regarded as tentative approximations not yet fully validated.

Part of our data are summarized in Table 1.2. It may be seen that Luganda is the language understood by the largest percentage of the country.

TABLE 1.2: *Percentages of Ugandans able to hold a conversation in Swahili, Luganda and English.*

	Swahili	Luganda	English
Men	52	51	28
Women	18	28	13
Total	35	39	21

But these figures include the 16 per cent of the population who speak Luganda as a first language. As a second language Swahili is spoken by a far higher percentage.

Many more men than women learn a second language. This fact is revealed by the differences in the percentages of men as opposed to women speaking Swahili and Luganda. A slightly larger number of men speak Swahili than speak Luganda, even when the native speakers of Luganda are included.

English is known by far fewer Ugandans than either of the other two languages. It is, of course, a language learned in school. For many people it is not much used in other circumstances, and tends to get forgotten. We can see this by considering the present ability to hold a conversation in English of those who have finished primary school (and therefore presumably could at one time converse in English). Figure 1.1 shows how the percentage falls as people get older and school is left further behind.

The relation between age (irrespective of schooling) and knowledge of Swahili, Luganda and English is shown in Figure 1.2. It is apparent that knowledge of both Swahili and English is greater among the younger people (and therefore must have been increasing over the last 30 years). But the percentage of people who understand Luganda has slightly declined during the same period.

Swahili is sometimes thought to be the lingua franca of the poor and the less educated in Uganda, and English is seen as the language of the élite. While it is obviously true that knowledge of English is greatest among those who have received some higher education, we also have data to show that many educated people also know more Swahili. Figure 1.3 shows the percentage of each educational group who are able to converse in each language. Knowledge of

25

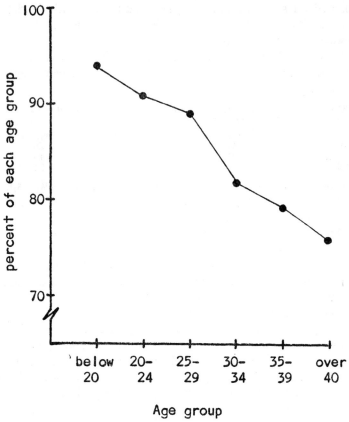

Figure 1.1: *Percentages of those who completed primary school and who can still understand a conversation in English.*

each of these languages increases with education, the increase for English being obviously the greatest.

A similar view of the relation between these languages may be obtained by considering the ability of different occupational groups to speak each language, as shown in Figure 1.4. As might be expected from the previous figures, among housewives Luganda is the most widely spoken language; and teachers know English best. But Swahili is the language best known among each of the other groups, with the exception of the unskilled workers, who know slightly more Luganda. It should be noted that these are the most tentative of all the figures reported here, since they depend so much on our sample having had the correct proportion of each occupation in

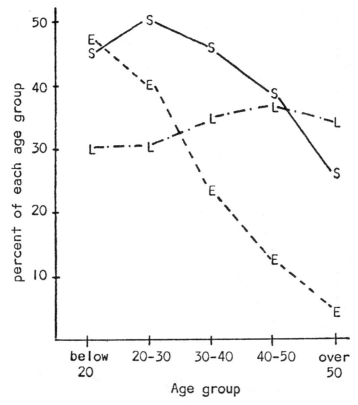

Figure 1.2: *Percentage of each group able to converse in Swahili (—S—), English (--E--), and Luganda (—·L·—).*

each district of Uganda. Since, for instance, 30 of the 51 teachers interviewed came from the Northern part of the country, the figure for the percentage of the teachers speaking Swahili may be too high.

In the course of our interviews we also asked several questions designed to elicit people's attitudes to different languages. The results are shown in Table 1.3. They should, however, be regarded with caution, as it became obvious when asking these questions that many people had not really thought about these matters. Thus when asked if English should remain the official language 82 per cent of the people said yes. But we got the impression that this was simply because they considered this to be a government matter, rather than because they held any strong views of their own. If the question

27

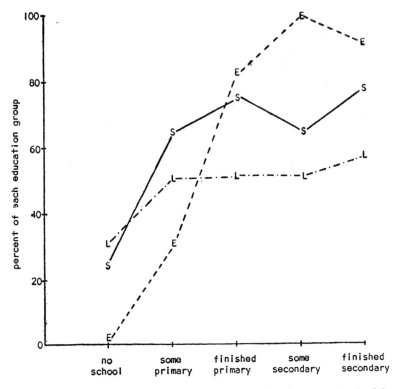

Figure 1.3: Percentage of each education group able to converse in Swahili (—S—), English (--E--), and Luganda (—·L·—).

TABLE 1.3: *Attitudes to Swahili, Luganda and English expressed as percentages. (Invalid answers lead to the figures not adding up to 100.)*

	English	Swahili	Luganda
Should English remain the official language? If not, what should be?	82	4	6
Which of English, Luganda, Swahili would you choose as the official language?	59	15	18
Which of English, Luganda, Swahili would you least like as the official language?	9	29	54
Relative rank in answer to questions above (see text).	1.4	2.2	2.4
Which language should children be taught to read and write in schools?	37	4	13
If all children in Uganda had to learn to read and write one language, what should it be?	41	7	7

28

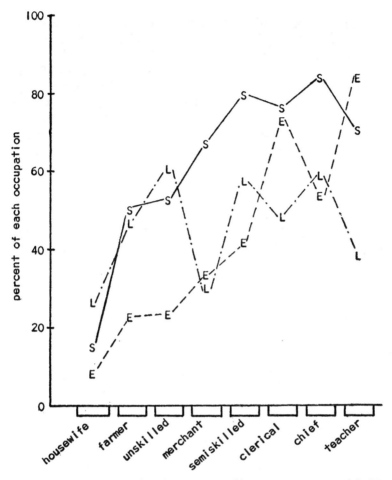

Figure 1.4:   *Percentage of each occupation able to converse in Swahili (S), English (E), and Luganda (L).*

were phrased in a slightly different way, with more emphasis being put on personal choice, then only 59 per cent favoured English. Those who preferred Luganda were mainly Baganda. When we tried to find out which of the three languages was least popular, it was clear that people living outside Buganda would be most unwilling to have Luganda as a national language. The fourth row of figures combines the two previous questions so as to show the average rank of each of the three languages with respect to the three possibilities, first, second and third most popular.

29

We also asked questions about the languages people wanted to be used in schools. Again, many people found these to be difficult questions to answer; they expected decisions of this kind to be taken by teachers. As may be seen from the last two rows of figures in Table 1.3, those who answered preferred English, the percentage increasing slightly when the question was worded so as to suggest that there might be one language taught in all schools throughout the country. But in addition (a point not noted in Table 1.3 where three languages are being compared) when asked 'Do you think Swahili should be taught as a subject in schools?' 81 per cent of the country answered yes.

Finally it should be remembered that all these data should be viewed with reserve. If the government wished to change its language policy, there is no doubt that language attitudes would also change. These are, however, political speculations which are outside the realm of this book.

PART 2

The Languages of Uganda

Before one can say how many languages there are in Uganda, one must know which languages are just different dialects, and which dialects are really very dissimilar and might be considered to be separate languages. But this cannot be done because there is no agreed way of defining what is meant by a language as opposed to a dialect. Generally speaking, differences between languages are larger than differences between dialects; and very often two groups of people are said to speak different languages when they differ not only in the way that they speak, but also in some other way, such as belonging to separately organized social or political groups. But there is no known way of determining on linguistic grounds alone when the difference between two speech forms is sufficiently great to require them to be regarded as different languages. Accordingly, in this part of the book, when we first start making linguistic comparisons, it should be remembered that what is called a language might well have been called a dialect, and vice versa.

Although there are no current official statements which list all the languages of Uganda, there are the official census reports which list the different tribes; and these same reports state that membership of a given tribe was largely determined by language. The last census which reported tribal data was in 1959. It recognized 32 Ugandan tribes and a number of non-Ugandan groups. The map published by the Lands and Surveys Department on the basis of the census data shows 31 of these tribes (omitting the Batwa, a small tribe of about 3,000 people), and in the attached notes mentions eight other tribes which were not separately enumerated in the census. This makes a total of 40 Ugandan tribes named in official publications.

In our own work we have found it convenient to name a slightly larger number of languages and dialects. Map 1 shows the approximate locations of 63 languages or dialects which we considered. After presenting our data we shall state an arbitrary criterion for the degree of similarity between two speech forms which is necessary for them to be considered to be merely dialects of the same language.

The map does not show the boundaries between the languages for two reasons. In the first instance some languages blend into others as one moves from the area central to one to the area central to the other. Thus it is possible to say that the people around Mbarara speak Runyankore and the people around Fort Portal speak Rutooro; but as one moves along the road from one of these towns to the other one will find that near the border between Ankole and Toro Districts there are villages where most of the people speak a dialect which is intermediate between Runyankore and Rutooro. And as one moves from this area back to the towns one finds other speech forms which are intermediate between this dialect and the town forms; and so on down to yet finer divisions between speech forms. This kind of dialect continuum seems to be common in most of the Bantu speaking areas of Uganda.

The second reason for not drawing boundaries on Map 1 applies more in cases where two completely distinct languages are next to one another. In Bukedi District, for example, there are villages where the majority of the population speak Lugwere next to villages where the majority of the population speak Ateso. But we cannot say there is a boundary between these two groups of villages. In each group there will be a large number of people whose first language is not that of the majority. Most of these, and many of the majority group as well, will be to some extent bilingual. It would be misleading to draw a line which suggests that there is a definite area where each of these languages is spoken.

HISTORICAL COMPARISONS

Linguists often speak of languages in terms of language families. When they do this they are usually acting on the assumption that groups of people, who now speak different languages, were previously part of the same group and spoke in much the same way in earlier times. In this view different languages were once merely different dialects which have diverged more and more in the course of time, until they have come to be regarded as different languages.

Starting on this basis, there are clearly two distinct groups of languages in Uganda: the Bantu languages in the South, and the

Nilo-Saharan languages in the North.* Nobody has ever shown any relation between these two groups of languages; there is no reason to think that their forerunners were ever related forms of the same language. Among the Nilo-Saharan languages of the North, many linguists would also doubt whether the Sudanic languages in the extreme North-West were in any way related to the Nilotic languages in other parts of the North. They would therefore say that there are three separate language families in Uganda.

Continuing the dividing process, it is generally agreed that the Nilotic languages in Uganda fall into two groups, now often called Western and Eastern Nilotic. These two groups used to be called Nilotic and Nilohamitic by linguists who doubted that they had more than a superficial similarity. But most experts now hold that their forerunners were similar dialects which diverged a long time ago, so that they are now quite distinct but distantly related. We may therefore say that the language families represented in Uganda are shown in Figure 2.1.

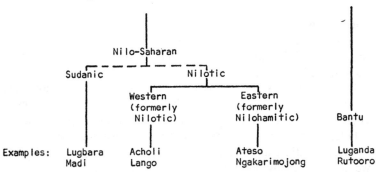

Figure 2.1: *Language families represented in Uganda. The dashed line linking Sudanic and Nilotic under the heading Nilo-Saharan indicates a relationship suggested by some linguists but doubted by others.*

It should be remembered that this figure indicates presumed historical relationships between languages. But it does not necessarily reflect historical relationships between tribes. In general, anthropologists and administrators have tended to define tribes in terms of groups of people speaking the same language, and to say that two tribes are related if they speak similar languages.

*The terminology used here is mainly that suggested by Greenberg. For discussions of the classification of African languages, see Greenberg (1963), Guthrie (1948, 1967), Fodor (1966), Tucker and Bryan (1956, 1966).

But we do not know if, for example, the Madi were ever a single tribe; and, if they were, we do not know if they ever shared a culture with the Lugbara. Similarly, despite the fact that Acholi and Lango are closely related languages, we cannot infer anything about the relations between the peoples who speak these languages. In fact, it is often claimed that the Langi are more like the Iteso; it is only their language that is of the Western Nilotic type. There certainly are many examples of an immigrant group losing their own language completely, and taking over that of the original inhabitants. We are not sure if this happened in the case of the Langi; but it seems fairly certain that something of this kind must have happened in the case of the Bahima, who are part of the Banyankore and speak a Bantu language very similar to that of the other Banyankore groups. They are said to have been a cattle keeping people who migrated from somewhere up in the North. Historians suggest that about three centuries ago they conquered the other Banyankore groups and came to live where they are now. At that time the Bahima were probably speaking a Nilotic or Hamitic language; but very little trace of this remains in their present speech. They now have a dialect very similar to the tribe they conquered; and as there are strong social and political pressures towards unification, they are becoming no longer identifiable as a tribe.

Because of mixtures of this kind, and because we do not know enough about the past relations between the tribal groupings in Uganda, the historical method is not very useful in trying to make a detailed classification of the languages of Uganda. Furthermore, in most practical discussions of the linguistic situation in Uganda, we are not really interested in the historical relations between languages; we are far more concerned with measures of the degree of similarity or of mutual intelligibility.

COMPARISONS OF SOUND SYSTEMS

There are many other ways of making comparisons between languages. Firstly one can compare the sound systems. Every language may be said to have a fairly small set of sounds which it uses for distinguishing one word from another. One of the most useful ways of comparing languages is to compare these sets of sounds. Comparisons of this kind can be used not only for indicating the distances between languages, but also for practical predictions of pronunciation difficulties. When speakers of a language sucn as Luganda do not have a difference corresponding to the difference in the English sounds in words such as *ship* and *sheep*, then one can predict that they will have difficulty in learning to pronounce words differentiated by these sounds.

The sound systems of the Bantu languages of Uganda are remarkably similar. In all of them syllables always end with a vowel (so that words such as **Luganda** and **Kampala** can be divided into **lu- ga- nda** and **ka- mpa- la**); and in nearly all of them there are five contrasting vowels, **i, e, a, o, u**. Phoneticians have found that it is very difficult to give helpful descriptions of vowels in terms of the actual positions of the tongue and lips; but they can be described in terms of two major aspects of their auditory quality. One of these aspects (which can be heard as the apparent pitch when vowels are whispered) distinguishes between what we may call front vowels as in English *he* and back vowels as in English *who*. The other (which can sometimes be heard as an overtone pitch when vowels are said on a very low pitch) distinguishes between what we may call high vowels, again as in English *he* (which is therefore both front and high) and low vowels as in English *had* (which contains a fairly low front vowel).

Figure 2.2(a) shows the relative quality of the vowels in a Bantu language such as Luganda in these terms. Two additional vowels are found in a few languages in the extreme west of Uganda, such as Rukonjo and Rwamba. Both these vowels are shown in parenthesis in Figure 2.2(a). One of them is intermediate in quality between **i** and **e** (phonetic symbol **ɩ**) and the other is between **u** and **o** (phonetic symbol **ɷ**).

The relative quality of some comparable English vowels is shown in Figure 2.2(b), which is drawn to the same (arbitrary) scale as Figure 2.2(a).

English has a much larger number of vowels than any Ugandan language. In addition to the 12 sounds shown in Figure 2.2(b) there are also different sounds in words such as *buy, bough, boy, beer, bare* and (for some speakers) other words as well. Furthermore, many of the English sounds differ not only in quality (their relative position on the chart), but also in that they are diphthongal (involving a change in quality during the vowel, and hence representation by a line not a point on the chart). The English diphthongs are

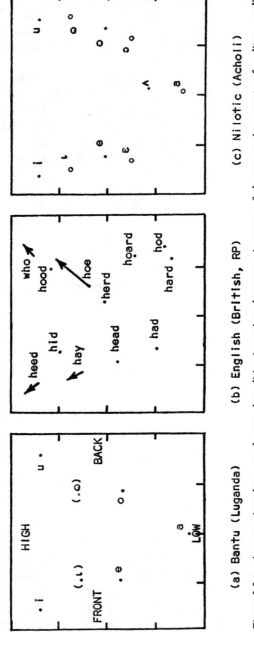

(a) Bantu (Luganda) (b) English (British, RP) (c) Nilotic (Acholi)

Figure 2.2: *A comparison between the vowel qualities in various languages in terms of the two major aspects of auditory quality (high-low and front-back) recognized by phoneticians. The diagrams are drawn to the same scale, so that the position of a point on one diagram indicates where it would be on the other diagrams. In the Nilotic languages the 10 vowels can be divided into two sets, one marked with solid points and the other with open circles.*

longer than the corresponding monophthongs (sounds with no major change in quality).

In most of the Ugandan Bantu languages there is a distinction between short and long vowels. Thus Luganda distinguishes between **kukula** (to grow) and **kukuula** (to pull out). But in nearly all these languages the long vowels are still monophthongs; there are only a few languages which have, in addition to the long and short vowels, diphthongs, as in Rutooro **amaizi** (water) and Runyankore **enya-maishwa** (animal). To some extent Ugandans tend to use the possible length difference between pairs such as **ii** and **i** to distinguish between English words such as *heed* and *hid*.

It is a feature of nearly all Ugandan Bantu languages that vowels are always long when they occur before a prenasal consonant such as **mb** or **nd**. Following this rule the first vowel in **Kampala** must be long, and so must the second in **Luganda**. In these languages there is also a rule lengthening vowels when they occur after consonant clusters with **y** or **w**, as in the second syllable in **omwana** (child). But there is yet another rule that says that, despite any lengthening due to previous rules, vowels are always short before double conso-nants. By this rule the first vowel in **bajja** (they came) is short, despite the fact that the pronoun is **ba**, and this combined with **a**, the past tense of the verb, normally produces a long vowel. Similarly the first vowel in **nnywedde** (I have drunk) is short (despite the lengthening effect of the **w**).

In the non-Bantu languages the vowel systems are much more complicated. In all of the Sudanic languages (Lugbara, Madi), the Western Nilotic group (Acholi, Lango, Alur, Dhopadhola) and the Eastern Nilotic group (Ateso, Ngakarimojong, Kakwa) there are nine or ten different vowel qualities; and in addition all these languages have contrasts between long and short vowels. These vowels can usually be divided into two sets of four or five vowels which may be symbolized: **i, e, ʌ, o, u** and **ɪ, ɛ, a, ɔ, ɷ**. In general the vowels of the second set are intermediate in quality between those of the first set, as illustrated in Figure 2.2(c). Thus Northerners have a larger number of vowels in their languages in comparison with Bantu speakers. This may in part account for the fact that they are often said to have a better pronunciation of English.

In the Nilotic languages there is not only a difference in quality between pairs such as **i** and **ɪ**, which is rather like the difference in quality between the vowels in *heed* and *hid* in English; there is also

37

another kind of difference which is more difficult for non-native speakers to learn. This difference in voice quality is due to the way in which the vocal cords vibrate. The orthographies of most of the Nilotic languages do not distinguish between these pairs of sounds, perhaps because there is a strong tendency for words to have vowels all of one kind or all of the other (a phenomenon known as vowel harmony). Even sophisticated native speakers of Acholi or Ateso find it hard to supply examples of the contrasts. But the differences are plainly there.

In comparison with the vowel systems, the consonant systems of Ugandan languages are more difficult to compare with each other and with English because they differ in a much larger number of ways. Basically, in describing consonants, we have to state the place of articulation (the location of the speech organs which approach or touch one another) and the manner of articulation (the way in which the speech organs approach or touch one another); but there are also other factors which will have to be considered.

As with the vowels, the consonant systems of the Bantu languages within Uganda all have a great deal in common. For each of them there are basically the four places of articulation described by phoneticians as labial (made with the lips), alveolar (made with the tongue articulating just behind the upper front teeth), palatal (the body of the tongue raised, and the blade of the tongue approaching or touching the front part of the palate in the roof of the mouth), and velar (the back of the tongue approaching or touching the soft palate at the back of the mouth). These four places of articulation may be illustrated by the sounds **b, d, j, g** (where the symbols have approximately the same values as in the English words *bay, day, jay, gay*).

There are also four basic manners of articulation: stop, nasal, fricative, and approximant. These articulations are exemplified by the sounds **b, m, v, w** (with the symbols having approximately the same values as in the English words *bet, met, vet, wet*). In a stop the articulators (the two lips, for **b**) are completely together, and no air comes out through the nose. In a nasal (such as **m**) there is a similar articulatory closure (the two lips for **m**), but the nasal air passages are open so that air can come out through the nose. In a fricative (such as **v**) the articulators are obstructing the air flow, the two lips (or the lower lip and the upper teeth) being close to one another, but not completely together. For an approximant (such as **w**) the articulators approach one another but do not obstruct the air flow to any considerable extent. Sometimes a stop consonant may be immediately followed by a fricative sound made at the same place of articulation. When this occurs (as it usually does for palatal stops), the sound may be called an affricate.

The possible combinations of these places and manners of articulation which occur in Luganda (and in many other Ugandan Bantu languages) are shown in Figure 2.3. In this figure the letters **ny** are used for a single sound, something like that in the middle of English *onion* or French *agneau*. The symbol ŋ indicates the sound at the end of English *sing*. This sound is not very common in Luganda; when it does occur it is always at the beginning and not at the end of a syllable as it is in English. The sound symbolized **j** always has a fricative component following it, and may be classified as a palatal affricate.

	labial	alveolar	palatal	velar
stop	b	d	j	g
nasal	m	n	ny	ŋ
fricative	v	z		
approximant	w	l	y	

Figure 2.3: The basic articulatory possibilities in the Luganda consonant system. The gaps in the chart indicate sounds which cannot occur in Luganda.

Many of these basic articulatory possibilities can occur in various forms. For all the stops and fricatives there are both voiced sounds (as in Figure 2.3) and voiceless sounds, in which the vocal cords are not vibrating; these voiceless sounds may be exemplified by the sounds **p, t, c, k** (where the symbols have approximately the same values as in the English words *pill, till, chill, kill* with **c** being used for something like the usual pronunciation of *ch*). Nasals and approximants are always voiced in Ugandan languages.

Both the voiced and voiceless stops and the voiced and voiceless fricatives also have forms in which they are preceded by a nasal, as in the syllables **mba, mpa, mva, mfa, nga.** The spelling **ng** usually

39

D

indicates a syllable beginning with a nasal before a g; this sound is much more common than the sound ŋ mentioned previously.

In Luganda (but not in most other Ugandan languages) the stops, fricatives, and nasals can occur as long consonants at the beginning of a syllable: there are words such as **ssatu** (three) and **tta** (kill!) where the intial consonant is longer and often more forceful than usual. In addition, in all the Ugandan Bantu languages, many of the single consonants can be followed by a **w** or a **y**, producing combinations such as **by, bw,** etc. All these combinatory possibilities are illustrated by means of a branching diagram in Figure 2.4 which lists all the labial consonants which occur in Luganda.

It will be readily apparent that a number of these possibilities do not occur in English; nor, as we shall see, do they all occur in the Northern Ugandan languages. With the possible exception of the long consonants, none of these sounds seems difficult for speakers of Northern Ugandan languages or English to learn. Prenasalized

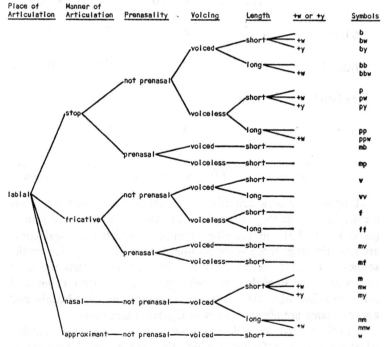

Figure 2.4:   A branching diagram illustrating all the contrasting labial consonants which actually occur in Luganda.

40

sounds do not occur in most of the Northern languages, but speakers of these languages (and speakers of English) usually learn to pronounce them in Bantu languages without much trouble.

There are, however, one or two difficulties for speakers of Ugandan Bantu languages who wish to learn English. In the first place there are major gaps, principally in the set of fricatives and in the set of approximants. Where English has four fricative sounds, as in *fin, thin, sin, shin,* most Eastern Ugandan Bantu languages have only two, **f** and **s**. Some of the Western languages have a third somewhat like English *sh*. But no Ugandan Bantu language has all four of these fricative sounds. Consequently the Eastern Ugandan Bantu have to learn to produce some form of *sh* sound which is distinct from *s*; and all the Ugandan Bantu have to learn to produce both a voiced and a voiceless dental fricative—the sounds at the beginnings of English words such as *this* and *thin*. The only Ugandan Bantu language with anything approaching either of these sounds is Lusoga, which has a voiced dental stop, written **dh** in the Lusoga orthography used for the early Lusoga Bible. But even here there are pronunciation problems for the language learner, as Lusoga has no contrast between this sound and the sound normally represented by **d**.

The remaining major gap in the consonant systems of Ugandan Bantu languages arises from the fact that none of them uses the difference between *r* and *l* for distinguishing between words. In the Luganda standard orthography there is a convention whereby **r** is written after the front vowels, **i, e**, and **l** is written elsewhere. But the sound is usually somewhere between **r** and **l**, and is not as predictable as the convention would indicate. Learning the English distinction between these two sounds is a well known difficulty.

Mention should also be made of another obvious difference between English and Ugandan Bantu consonants. In English, consonants can be initial or final in a syllable; and in each place many combinations are possible. There are nearly 100 ways of beginning a word in English, and about half as many again of ending one. But in Ugandan Bantu languages consonants can be only initial in a syllable; and there are nothing like so many possible sequences of consonants. Complex sequences such as those at the beginning of *stray* and the end of *sixth* are new to speakers of Ugandan Bantu languages, and have to be learnt.

The consonant systems of the Northern group of languages are very different from those of the Bantu languages; and they are also very different from one another. In our brief discussions of the vowel systems of these languages we were able to consider all of them together; but this cannot be done for the consonant systems.

In the Sudanic languages (Lugbara and Madi) there are several sounds not found elsewhere in Uganda, or in English. These include the sounds written gb and kp, which are simultaneous articulations of g and b, and k and p (and hence are called labial velars). There are also laryngealized (glottalized) sounds 'b 'd 'w 'y in which a kind of glottal catch (symbolized ') accompanies the normal articulation of b d w y. The gb and kp are similar to the sounds occurring in Nigerian languages such as Igbo; and the laryngealized sounds are similar to those occurring in other Nigerian languages such as Hausa. A full description of these sounds may be found elsewhere.*

The Sudanic languages also have sounds articulated in a larger number of places. The Lugbara sounds t and d are made with the tongue touching the teeth (a dental articulation) rather than just behind them (an alveolar articulation) as in most other Ugandan languages; accordingly these sounds are symbolized t+ and d+ in phonetic transcriptions. When these d sounds occur in combination with s and z they are articulated just behind the teeth, in the alveolar region; and when they occur with r they are articulated still further back, in the post-alveolar region. The fricative quality of the combinations with r is not common elsewhere. The combinations ts, dz, tr, dr, are known as affricates. The basic set of Lugbara consonants is shown in Figure 2.5. All the stops, affricates, and

	labial	dental	alveolar	post-alveolar	palatal	velar	labial-velar
stop	b	d+				g	gb
affricate			dz	dr			
fricative	v	z					
nasal	m		n		ny		
approximant			l	ɼ	y		w
laryngealized stop or approximant	'b	'd			'y		'w

Figure 2.5: *The basic set of Lugbara consonants. For each of the sounds in the first three rows there is a voiceless counterpart (viz: p, t, k, kp, ts, tr, f, s); and for each of the sounds in the first two rows there is a nasal compound counterpart (viz: mb, nd, ndz, ndr, ŋg, mŋgb). Lugbara also has h and ' (a glottal stop).*

*See Ladefoged (1968).

42

fricatives have voiceless counterparts; and all the stops and affricates have nasal compound counterparts. It may be seen that Lugbara uses a comparatively large number of places of articulation, and some extra manners of articulation, all of which provide pronunciation difficulties for speakers of other languages.

The consonant systems of the Western and Eastern Nilotic languages are much simpler. The basic set for all of them is shown in Figure 2.6. Nearly all these languages have four places of articulation; and at each of them there is a voiced stop, a voiceless

	labial	alveolar	palatal	velar
voiceless stops	p	t	c	k
voiced stops	b	d	j	g
nasals	m	n	ny	ŋ
fricatives	f v	s		
approximants	w	l, r	y	

Figure 2.6: *The consonant systems of: (a) Western Nilotic languages such as Lango and Acholi; (b) Eastern Nilotic languages such as Ateso. The sounds f and v (or their variants pf/bv) occur only in (a), and the sound s occurs only in (b).*

stop, and a nasal. The stop made in the palatal position, **c**, is accompanied by some friction and might be better regarded as an affricate. The main deficiencies in comparison with English and other languages are among the fricatives. Apart from the sounds in loan words, the Western Nilotic languages have only labial fricatives (which are often realized as affricatives **pf, bv**), and the Eastern Nilotic languages have only **s** (or, as an alternant in Ngakarimojong, a voiceless dental fricative: **th**). In Dhopadhola, there is also a set of dental sounds (usually realized as the voiced and voiceless fricatives **dh** and **th**) which no longer occur in the other Ugandan languages in this group. In addition to the sounds shown in Figure 2.6 there are consonant clusters with **w** in both groups of languages and with y in the Western group. Both groups of languages also have a variant of **t** in between vowels which is something like the voiced alveolar tap which is the realization of *t* in between vowels in American English in words such as *butter*. This sound may be heard in the name: Obo*t*e.

Finally, in this brief characterization of the sound systems, mention must be made of the relative pitch on which words are said. All languages use pitch changes to produce differences in meaning. Some, like English and Swahili, use them only for syntactic purposes, such as differentiating between questions and statements. But others including all the Ugandan languages, use them not only in this way but also for distinguishing between words. Thus in Luganda the word **kuwola** means 'to borrow' if it is said with the first syllable low and the other two high, but it means 'to grow cold' if it is said with the tones low-high-low. In the Ugandan Bantu languages there are not many words where changes of pitch will produce a change in meaning of this kind. But nevertheless each word has a characteristic pattern of pitches. Producing a wrong pitch pattern will always result in the word being heard as mispronounced, even if it does not change it into a word with another meaning.

Pitch characterizes words in Ugandan Bantu languages in much the same way as stress characterizes words in English. There are a few words such as the verbs (*to*) *produce* and (*to*) *insult* and the nouns (*the*) *produce* and (*the*) *insult* where changing the stress pattern changes the meaning; but every polysyllabic word has its characteristic stress pattern. It would sound very odd to say *photographer* with the same stress pattern as *photographic*. But this analogy between tone in Uganda and stress in English cannot be pushed too far. In English, as the examples given show, changes in the stress do not change the underlying meaning of the stem of a word; they affect only its grammatical function. Whereas in Bantu languages pitch can change the meaning of the stem of a word, as well as change the grammatical function.

Probably in most of the Ugandan Bantu languages, each vowel in a word has to be marked as having one of two basic pitch possibilities (tones). Where there are long vowels they can each have two pitches which are the same or they can each have two different pitches, as long as the first is a high pitch and the second a low pitch. In this way gliding pitches from high to low are possible. A falling pattern of this kind can occur within a single vowel, and might be considered a third tone. Rising pitches from low to high have not been observed as characterizing any words. Nasal consonants also have distinctive tones on some occasions; and the Luganda long consonants act as if the first of each pair has replaced a vowel, and therefore has to be assigned a characteristic tone.

In English there are rules governing stress changes: nouns like *produce, insult, survey, torment* can be derived from the corresponding verbs by a rule which states that to form a noun from a verb the stress must be moved to the first syllable of the word. Similarly, in Ugandan languages, the grammatical tone changes probably could be stated entirely in terms of rules (but no one has yet formulated a complete set of rules). For example, consider the data in Table 2.1.*

There is a relation between the forms on the left with an initial vowel and the forms on the right without. Nearly all words in Luganda belong to one or other of two classes from the point of view of their tonal behaviour. The words in the first two lines of examples belong to the first tone class. For these words, the general rule is that the tone pattern must be the same in both sets of words, irrespective of whether there is an initial vowel or not. The sequence of low and high tones is kept the same by moving the tones from one syllable to the next. So, in the first and second examples, words

TABLE 2.1: *Some Luganda tonal changes. High tone is marked with an acute accent thus : á; low tone with a grave accent: à; and falling tone with a circumflex: â. (Rising tones do not occur within a syllable.)*

Citation Forms		Predicative Forms	
Luganda	English	Luganda	English
1. èkítábó	a book	kìtábó	It is a book
2. òmúntú	a man	mùntú	He is a man
3. òmùkázì	a woman	mùkázì	She is a woman
4. òmùwéèsí	a blacksmith	mùwéèsí	He is a blacksmith
5. èkìgérè	a foot	kìgèrê	It is a foot
6. òmùwóòzá	a tax gatherer	mùwóózà	He is a tax gatherer

which are low, high, high, (high) remain with the first syllable low and the remainder high, even when there is no initial vowel. Consequently in the first word, the syllable **-ki** has a high tone when there is an initial vowel and a low tone when there is not. The words in the third and fourth line belong to the second tone class. For these words the general rule is that the tones on each syllable remain the same irrespective of whether there is an initial vowel or not. The words in the fifth and sixth lines belong to a comparatively

*These rules and data derive from the work of Dorothy Galer.

small group of words which have a similar tone pattern to those of the second tone class in the citation forms. But their predicative forms are generated by the rule that applied to the first tone class. The tone pattern in the fifth line keeps the same shape (low, low, high, low; or low, low, falling) by moving the tones from one syllable to the next, so that the syllable -ge has a high tone when there is an initial vowel and a low tone when there is not. In the sixth word there are some additional changes. By our general rule of keeping the tone pattern the same (low, low, high, low) we would have got ***mùwòózá†**. But this form has a syllable with a rising tone: **-wòó**, which is not permitted in Luganda. Accordingly we must add another widely applicable rule, namely: if any tone rule leads to a long vowel having a rising tone, then change the low tone on the first part of it to a high tone, making one long high tone. These rules are slightly oversimplified as given; but they illustrate the kind of statements that can be made.

SYNTACTIC COMPARISONS‡

It is very difficult to compare the sentence patterns that can occur in different languages. We were able to compare the sound systems because the sounds of all the languages in the world can be described in terms of a limited number of phonetic features. But there is no similar way of comparing sentence patterns. Accordingly, in this section we shall simply outline some of the chief characteristics of the Ugandan Bantu languages. We can say nothing systematic about any of the Northern languages except to point out that they do not have these characteristics.

The Bantu languages of Uganda have in the main the same syntactic features found in Bantu languages in general. If the Ugandan languages are outstanding in any way, it may be in possessing more of the entries from the standard set of Bantu characteristics than do most other groups of Bantu languages. The most distinctive grammatical feature of the Bantu languages is the extensive system of class concords, or prefixes which occur before the stems of nouns and many other classes of words. Thus one form of the Luganda word for 'man' is **muntu**; the stem is **-ntu** and the prefix which marks it as being one of the class of singular

†In accordance with the usual linguistic conventions an asterisk before the word denotes a hypothetical form.
‡This section includes material supplied to us by Carol Scotton.

living beings is **mu-**. The corresponding plural form is **bantu**, the stem being the same and the prefix **ba-** indicating membership of the plural class of living beings. The same stem occurs in **kintu** (thing) and **bintu** (things), **ki-** and **bi-** being the singular and plural prefixes for the classes of inanimate objects. Bantu scholars have set up a system in which the original Bantu noun classes are numbered from 1 to 23. Table 2.2 shows some of the prefixes which have been reconstructed and the corresponding present day Luganda prefixes, when they are different. The prefixes used in other Ugandan languages are similar, but different languages have lost different classes in their evolution from the original form of the Bantu language.

TABLE 2.2: *The forms of the prefixes for some of the original Bantu noun classes. The corresponding Luganda prefix is also shown in parentheses when it is different.*

Class Number	Singular	Plural	Rough underlying idea
1	mu		living beings (persons)
1a	—		personal names, titles, personifications
2		a (ba)	plurals of 1 and 1a
3	mu		living things and artifacts
4		mi	(trees, parts of the body, tools, utensils)
5	li / double consonant		things found in quantities or sets, mass nouns (fruits,
6		ma	stones, water)
7	ki		inanimate objects
8		vi (bi)	(things)
9	ni (n)		common objects, animals
10		li (n, zi)	
11	lu		objects with extension
12	ka		diminutives
13	tu		very smallest quantities (drop of water, pinch of salt)
14		vu (bu)	diminutives, abstractions
15	ku		verb infinitives
16	pa (wa)		locative, relatively near or central
17	ku		locative, relatively far or going towards
18	mu		locative, encirclement, or going into
20	ghu (gu)		augmentation
22		gha (ga)	

The classes match up, for the most part, with one class as the regular plural of another class. In some cases, one class is the plural counterpart of more than one singular class. Some scholars have attempted to attach semantic significance to the natural groupings of nouns by classes. In general, such significance is not uniformly present in any Bantu language. Certain classes, however, do seem to include mainly certain classes of objects. Table 2.2 gives an indication of some of these groupings which occur in Ugandan Bantu languages.

The prefix system has been likened by most scholars to the sex gender systems found in other languages in the world, notably in some European languages such as Latin, French, or German. As in sex gender systems, modifiers agree with their nouns in the Bantu languages. However, the Bantu noun class system probably affects the syntactic structure more than any system of sex gender classes, for the degrees of differentiation are more numerous; there are up to 20 separate sets of class concords in Bantu languages compared to two or three sex gender classes in other languages. Further, the system affects a greater variety of grammatical classes of words, including not only nouns and adjectives, but also numerals, demonstratives, and personal pronouns. Table 2.3 illustrates some of the agreements which occur in Luganda. It may be seen that the Bantu system of concord is, for the most part, alliterative. For example, all forms appearing in concord with a noun in the ki- class in Luganda will also have a ki- in the prefix.

TABLE 2.3: *The Luganda concord system for the first nine noun classes*

Class Prefixes (with initial vowel)   Concord Prefixes (without initial vowel)

Roots and Stems used as Nouns		Roots and Stems used as Adjectives		Numerals 1–5 and -meka		Pronominal Roots, Verbs and Particles	
Sing.	Plur.	Sing.	Plur.	Sing.	Plur.	Sing.	Plur.
omuntu (man)		mu-		o-		o-	
	abantu		ba-		ba-		ba-
omuti (tree)		mu-		gu-		gu-	
	emiti		mi-		e-		gi-
erinnya (name)		li-		li-		li-	
	amannya		ma-		a-		ga-
ekintu (thing)		ki-		ki-		ki-	
	ebintu		bi		bi-		bi-
ente (cow)		n-		e-		e-	
	ente		n-		-		gi- zi-

A second notable characteristic of Ugandan Bantu languages is the disyllabic noun prefix (in effect, a double prefix) which varies according to noun class. The presence or absence of the pre-prefix signals certain syntactic relations, such as the definiteness of the noun. For example, compare Luganda **Oyagala okugula emmeeza**? 'Do you want to buy the table?' with **Oyagala kugula mmeeza**? 'Do you want to buy a table?' Much research remains to be done on the exact role of the pre-prefix in syntactic relations. Many Bantu languages in other areas have lost the pre-prefix, but not those in Uganda. The disyllabic prefix appears in its fullest form in Lumasaba, where each of the two syllables of the noun prefix often has a consonant.

Ugandan Bantu languages show the same favourite sentence types as Bantu languages in general. In some cases they are quite similar to English sentence types, but quite different in other cases. The normal Bantu sentence type is Noun Phrase + Verb Phrase (in that order, as in English). A variation on this type not found in English consists of a noun phrase which is a locative nominal (the kind of construction which would function adverbially in English) plus a verb phrase which is in agreement with the nominal, as usual. For example, in Luganda **Ku bbalaza kwange kwayiiseeko amazzi** 'Some water has been spilt on my veranda', the verb **kwayii-seeko** agrees in prefix with the locative nominal **Ku bbalaza,** as does the possessive adjective **kwange** 'my'. The locative nominal generally has no independent morphological existence of its own; that is, it is normally formed from the base of a noun of another class with the addition of prefixes which mark it as a locative. Various enclitics to the verb also mark the locative construction. Another favourite Bantu sentence type not found in English but widely used in the Ugandan Bantu languages consists of a noun phrase standing alone as a sentence, as in Luganda **Gino miti** 'They (here) are trees'.

As in English, word order is extremely important in Bantu languages to mark syntactic relations. Thus in English we rely on word order to differentiate between the subject and object in sentences such as: *The boy hit the girl* and *The girl hit the boy.* Similarly, in Bantu languages the subject normally comes first, and the object comes after the verb. Sometimes the typical word order of subject + verb + object is lacking, and the presence of the object prefix in the verb assembly will identify definitely the object (provided the subject and object are not both of the same noun class and therefore showing the same object prefix).

In Bantu, few words consist of a root only which can be a 'free form', such as English *like, boy*. Rather, the majority of Bantu words are built up on bound forms (a form which cannot occur alone as a 'word') which are roots and become 'words' only with the addition of prefixes or suffixes or both. Thus, as we have seen, **-ntu** is a Bantu root. The addition of various prefixes makes it into various words. Luganda **omuntu** (man), **ekintu** (thing) and **obuntu** (existence) all come from this root.

The Bantu verbal assembly consists of a root, a large number of interdependently obligatory prefixes, optional prefixes and suffixes. The basic relationships of subject, tense or aspect, voice or mood, object identification, status of the verbal subject or object in a subordinate relative clause, are all signalled by prefixes attached to the verb root. Perhaps most notable to scholars used to European languages is the fact that negative and positive conjugations in the verb show different subject and tense/aspect prefixes.

An example of a possible verbal assembly in Luganda (but not likely because of its length) is **Bandibimunnyagiddengako** 'They would grab from him for me (repeatedly) the things'. **Ba-** 'they', **-ndi-** (conditional), **-bi-** 'things', **-mu-** 'him', **-n-** 'for me', **-nyagi-** (verb root) 'to grab', **-dde-** (tense), **-nga-** (repeated action), **-ko** 'from'.

One distinctive feature of the Bantu verb system is the possibility of deriving new verb stems by the addition of affixes. The form of the verb corresponding to what would be the passive in English is derived in this way. In addition, many other forms which would have to be expressed quite differently in English are simply derived forms in Ugandan Bantu languages. There are usually, for example, causative (causing the action to happen), associative (doing the action with or to another), frequentive (repeating the action), static (sustained action), intensive (action persisted), derived forms of the verb. The number of possible derived forms is large (probably up to 14 in Luganda, for example). These verbs can take any of the inflectional prefixes which occur with simple verb stems, but they control their own syntactic patterns. For example, a derived applied (sometimes called prepositional) form regularly governs two objects (one indirect and one direct), as in Luganda **Basekulira omwami kasooli** 'They are pounding maize for the chief'. The suffix **-ira** shows that the stem **-kul-** is being used in the applied form.

There are a large number of tense distinctions possible in Bantu languages; in general most of them occur in the Ugandan Bantu languages. Four degrees of past and future time can be signalled by a change in prefix in the verbal assembly, for example. Auxiliary

50

verbs are made use of to cover some compound tenses, with the verb 'to be' one of those used as an auxiliary. The verb -li- (to be) occurs, for example, in Luganda's far future tense form, **Tuliba(nga) tukyasoma** 'We shall still be reading (repeatedly)'.

From some points of view, it could be argued that articles and prepositions do not exist in Bantu languages. At least, the relationships signalled by these parts of speech in European languages are not signalled by self-standing forms in Bantu languages. Instead they are signalled mainly by affixes.

COMPARISONS OF INDIVIDUAL LANGUAGES

The net result of all the comparisons we have made so far still does not go much beyond the divisions made on historical grounds. Comparing the sound systems has given some indication of the degree of similarity within and between groups of languages; and particular features of one or two languages have also been mentioned. The syntactic notes do not go even this far. We have not given any detailed estimates of the degree of similarity of individual languages or dialects.

There are basically four ways in which individual languages can be compared. In the first place one can get the opinions of local people. Nobody knows all the languages in Uganda, but many people know several of the languages around them, and are willing to make statements about their relative similarity. Remarks of this kind are sometimes indicative of nothing other than an informant's belief; but they are sometimes very helpful.

A second and better way of estimating the degree of similarity between languages is to compare lists of words in each language. If we find the word conveying a particular meaning is very similar in two different languages it may be just chance (the Luganda word for 'egg' is **èggî**), or because of borrowing (the Luganda word for 'bus' is **bbasi**), or because they are historically related (the Luganda and the Swahili words for 'bee' are `njúkì` and **nyuki**). But whatever the reason for the similarity, it is possible to measure the degree of likeness between two languages by taking a list of meanings and counting the number of similar words which have the same area of meaning in the two languages.

A third technique for comparing languages is to measure the degree of phonetic similarity among words having the same meaning.

Thus the word for 'bone' in Luganda is **è`ggúmbà** and in Lukenyi is **èìgômbá**; these two words are more alike than either is like the Rukiga word with the same meaning, which is **èìgúfá**. These degrees of similarity can be expressed in terms of a phonetic scale.

Finally one can test the extent to which people actually understand another language. One way of doing this is to get a group to listen to a story told them in another language or dialect, and then see if they can answer questions about it. If a school child who has had no experience of a particular language nevertheless understands this language, it can only be because his own language (or some other language which he has learnt) is in some way similar to it.

The results of each of these four types of comparisons can be expressed in terms of numbers. Numerical estimates of similarity made by knowledgeable local people are probably not very reliable; different local experts will give different figures, and even the same man will give different estimates when the questions are put to him in a slightly different way on different occasions. But the other three techniques are more reliable and are valid indicators of similarity between languages. It is possible to make reasonably good estimates of the percentages of words in common, the degree of phonetic similarity, and the degree of comprehension of stories in another language. It is also possible to estimate whether the figures show statistically significant differences between languages, or whether they might have arisen by chance. It is sometimes said that one really knows something only when it can be expressed in terms of numbers which are valid, reliable and significant. We are well aware that in this scientific sense we cannot claim to know very much. Our fieldwork and experimental procedures are described below, together with some of the more technical aspects of our results. The general reader may omit the whole of this section. But it must be included so that our conclusions can be properly evaluated.

METHODOLOGY AND TECHNICAL DATA

INFORMED OPINION

During the course of our fieldwork we visited every district in Uganda, and talked to a large number of administrators, local chiefs, and other sources of informed opinion. We were also assisted by 12 Makerere students in part of their long vacation in April 1968.

Each of these fieldworkers travelled all over his native district and, in some cases, over the adjacent district as well. Sebei was the only district not visited by a student fieldworker speaking one of the local languages. The fieldworkers compiled word lists of the local languages (see below) and gathered opinions concerning the degree of similarity between these languages and the languages all around. They were told to find informants who knew the views of the community, and to ask them questions of the form 'How much can people around here understand of the such and such language?' They avoided using questions of the form 'How much can *you* understand . . .'

We did not succeed in getting a good set of questions which would elicit answers that could be standardized. Basically we tried to operate in terms of a five-point scale that showed whether people thought the neighbouring language was such that they could understand (1) none, (2) only a few words, (3) about half a conversation, (4) most that was said, (5) everything. We asked questions about different hypothetical situations, such as 'If someone preached a sermon in . . .; If someone told a story in . . .; If someone from such and such a place started working in this village . . .'. Appropriate answers on the five-point scale were suggested.

We knew that the best that this technique could do would be to give us the beliefs of a speech community concerning the degree of communication possible in other languages; and these beliefs might be biased. It has often been shown that the attitude of one group of people to another has an effect at least on their belief about the mutual intelligibility of their languages. When people think that their neighbours are inferior in some way they do not admit to understanding their language. But when they regard them as more advanced then they readily claim that they can understand them.

When the results of this part of the fieldwork were collated it was apparent that different fieldworkers were behaving in different ways. Consequently although their reports were indicative of similarities between languages and of beliefs that people held, they were not quantitatively reliable.

WORD LIST COMPARISONS

Transcriptions were made of the words corresponding to a list of at least 99 meanings as given by 47 speakers of Northern languages

53

or dialects, and a list of at least 94 meanings as given by 81 speakers of Bantu languages or dialects. For eight of the Northern languages and 20 of the Bantu languages the transcriptions were made by a linguist. The remaining lists were compiled by the 12 Makerere student fieldworkers who had been given a few days training in how to do this task. Their transcriptions were certainly unreliable in phonetic detail; but cross-checking indicated that most of them were satisfactory for showing whether a given meaning has a roughly similar or a definitely different form in each of the languages being compared. Many of the lists were so similar that there was no point in considering them all separately. In the comparisons to be reported below we used all the linguist's transcriptions and a further 12 lists compiled from the students' transcriptions of the Northern languages, and a further ten lists compiled from the students' transcriptions of the Bantu languages.

The list of meanings used went through a number of revisions before an appropriate form was evolved. Others doing work of this kind have used a 100 or 200 basic word list, carefully selected so as to be independent of any particular culture. But this is an unnecessary constraint when one is studying the degree of similarity of a limited group of languages whose speakers share many cultural phenomena. Thus elephants are known throughout Uganda, and are a proper subject of enquiry (but one would not, of course, ask questions about tigers or ice). The list still has to be balanced so that it does not reflect one aspect of the culture unduly. It would be unwise for it to consist entirely of a list of wild animal names; an agricultural people might have borrowed these and almost no others from their hunting neighbours. But, for assessing relative similarity, it does not matter if some of the words have been borrowed from another language or not, provided only that the list of meanings is likely to produce about the same proportion of loan words as occur in the language as a whole.

The basic vocabulary, which is theoretically more resistant to change through contact, may be the appropriate object of study for those concerned with historical relationships; but we did not need to limit ourselves in this way, since we were concerned with assessing present day possibilities of communication.

Because of the additional flexibility which was open to us for the choice of the meanings to be compared, we decided to set up a new list. Our guiding principle was to use meanings which elicited reliable answers (answers which did not differ from informant to informant for chance reasons) and which were valid indicators of the communicative possibilities of the language as a whole. Acting on this principle we were able to avoid many items which other investigators have used. We did not include items such as 'we, in, at, if, how', which are apt to be realized by diverse grammatical processes and may not exist as isolatable words which can be reliably given by informants. In addition, we tried to avoid using meanings which might lead to a number of equivalent forms, and which were therefore not reliable in that it is largely chance which determines which form is given by an informant. Thus for an English word like 'come' there may be two or three words each of which might be regarded by different investigators or different informants as the correct common equivalent in a given language. The following items had to be eliminated from our preliminary lists because there were no satisfactory general equivalents in many Ugandan languages: 'arrow, enemy, (to) finish, (to) grasp, (to) light a fire, (to) play, river, roof, (to) say, (to) sleep, (to) vanish, (to) wake up'. Conversely, to stick to our previous example, meanings such as 'elephant' were very useful. We did not find any Ugandan language which had more than one generic term for elephant. Some had additional specific terms for 'rogue elephant', etc.; but informants always recognized these as specifics and could be easily induced to give the general term.

We did not succeed in devising a list which is entirely free from cultural variations within the groups of languages being investigated. Often if we left the meaning we were looking for too vague we would be given some local specific term; and even if we specified that, for instance, by 'boy' we meant the term used to describe an eight-year-old male, we got different forms from neighbouring tribes, one of which had a circumcision ritual and the other of which did not. In such cases we were obviously recording cultural differences which were not necessarily good indicators of general language differences.

Another fault in the list is that one or two of the items should have been eliminated, as they did not produce independent words. We avoided using both 'bee' and 'honey' as we knew beforehand that they were often the same. But we now know that in many of the Northern languages 'feather' is equivalent to 'hair of bird', and in some languages 'wing' is simply 'arm of bird'.

There were additional difficulties in constructing a list of meanings

55

E

for use among closely related languages such as those in the Ugandan Bantu group. Several common words are virtually identical in all these languages, and consequently contribute nothing to measures of differentiation between the individual languages.

The complete list is given in Table 2.4. This table also shows the number of different forms which occurred in each of the 20 Bantu languages for which accurate transcriptions were available, and the number of these languages having each form. Thus the word for 'animal' occurred in four different forms, one of them occurring in 14 languages, another in three, another in two, and one form in only one language. This kind of comparison sometimes obscures similarities in that a language may use an uncommon form for a given meaning, but may nevertheless have the more common word in its vocabulary. Thus the Runyarwanda for 'finger' is **urutoke**, which is a form not found elsewhere in Uganda. The common form for 'finger' among the neighbouring Ugandan languages is **orukumu**. Runyarwanda has **urukumu**, but in this language it means, specifically, 'first finger'. Similarly to say that only two languages, Rwamba and Lubwisi, have the particular form **nyama** for 'animal', obscures the fact that many other languages use this form with the meaning 'meat'.

Similar forms in different languages having slightly different meanings occurred quite often; and it frequently proved confusing to informants who, after their own work was over, offered to help us by looking through previously compiled lists for other languages. They would often tell us that we had noted a word wrongly; and it was sometimes hard to convince them that another language might use a certain word such as **kugenda** for 'to go away' when from their point of view this word really meant 'to walk'. We do not know how to incorporate these facts most usefully in measures of language similarity. Nobody knows the part played in cross-language communication by the existence of similar words with slightly different meanings (such as *mutton* in English and *mouton* in French); without further research we would not like to say whether they help or confuse.

The technique used for comparing words is best illustrated by an example. Table 2.5 lists the words that were given for 'pig' in 20 Bantu languages. We have seen that words in these languages consist of a prefix plus a stem; and that a stem consists of repetitions of consonant-vowel-consonant-vowel, etc. Only stems were

56

TABLE 2.4: *List of meanings used in comparing Ugandan languages, examples (from particular languages) of the types of stem corresponding to each of them in the 20 Bantu languages listed in Table 2.5, and the number of these languages having a form similar to each of the cited stems. The first column shows the use that was made of each item: 1= used in comparing words in all languages; 2= used in Northern languages only; 3= used in Bantu languages only; 4= used in all languages and in phonetic comparisons of Bantu languages.*

Use	Meaning		Number out of the 20 Bantu languages having a form similar to each of the cited stems						
1	Animal	-sóló	14	-nyámáswà	3	-nyámá	2	-kóókó	1
1	Arm	-kónò	16	-bókò	3	-gálò	1		
1	Ash	-vú	10	-kóké	8	-shéndà	1	-syánù	1
1	Bear child (to)	-záálá	16	-ìbúlà	2	-búútá	1	-kóótà	1
4	Bee	-júkì	20						
4	Bird	-nyónyí	19						
1	Blood	-sáàyi	6	-ságámá	6	-fugi	3	-báángà	3
		-girá	1					-rásò	1
4	Bone	-ggúmbà	10	-tábàáná	3	-lénzì	2	-sindé	2
						-húŋú	1	-sigázi	1
1	Boy (8 years old)	-ójò	6	-séèrè	1	-pétà	1	-isùká	2
		-syánì	2	-jáálì	1				
4	Buffalo	-bògó	18	-zìmbá	6	-tòngólá	1		
1	Build (to)	-ómbèká	11	-hòìhóìlyà	3	-húgùhùgù	3	-lìkó	1
1	Butterfly	-wòjjòló	5	-nyúgùnyúgù	1	-kùrùkùrù	1	-ùlùkútù	3
		-yòyò	1	-sùmbá	1			-korokómbè	1
4	Buy (to)	-gúlá	19	-àndá	6	-sírìnzá	2	-bìfìró	2
1	Charcoal	-kálá	10	-rérì	6	-kákà			
1	Cloud	-cù	10	-bìldá	1				
4	Cooked (to be)	-hyá	19						
1	Cow	-té	14	-ŋóómbé	3	-kafú	3		
4	Crocodile	-ggóónyá	16	-pìyò	4				
4	Die (to)	-fà	19	-hòlà	1				
1	Dog	-bwá	18	-bwéni	2				
4	Drink (to)	-nywá	20						
4	Ear	-tù	19	-pókópó	1				
4	Eat	-lyá	20						
1	Egg	-ggì	12	-hùrì	7	-fyà	1		
1	Elbow	-kókòlà	16	-kùmbó	3	-jóòjò	1		

Build (to) — additional cited stems: -kwéra 1. Butterfly — additional cited stem: -búlùbúlù 2.

57

TABLE 2.4 (continued)

Number out of the 20 Bantu languages having a form similar to each of the cited stems

Use	Meaning	Form	No.	Form	No.	Form	No.	Form	No.
4	Elephant	-jóvú	9	-jòjò	5	-zógì	5	-bòngó	1
2	Eye	(Bantu data incomplete)							
1	Feather	-òyá	18	-bábá	1	-sárásárá	1	-tòkè	1
		-àlá	10	-kúmú	4	-gáló	3		
1	Finger	-búká	1					-nwé	1
4	Fire	-líró	18	-syò	1	-káárá	1	-nágè	1
1	Fish	-cú	7	-yényánjá	5	-ŋééní	5		
		-sámákè	1						
4	Flower	-múlí	17	-ákò	3	-ghánjá	2	-réŋgè	1
1	Foot	-gèrè	11	-gúlú	4				
		-kálá	1						
4	Frog	-kéré	17	-zé	1	-gbé	1	-sónsóniá	1
				-ishíkí	5	-káàná	5	-gúná	1
1	Girl (8 years old)	-wálá	6	-mbèsà	1			-kóóbwà	1
		-síiká	1						
4	Give (to)	-wá	18	-wèèryá	1	-pèlsya	1	-gyà	2
		-gééndá		-àbà	3	-cá	3		
1	Go away (to)	-gééndá	9	-hà	1			-tíìnà	1
		-bwáwò	1						
4	Goat	-bízí	17	-héné	2	-mèèmé	1	-sátsì	1
1	Hair	-vííří	8	-shòkyé	7	-zúné	2	-túmbú	1
		-síkámó	1						
1	Head	-twéé	19	-móó	1	-mvà	1	-ká	1
				-òwà	3				
				-òyò	7				
1	Hear (to)	-wúlírá	15						
1	Heart	-tímá	13						
4	Hen	-kókò	20						
1	Herd (to)	-rfísá	13	-àyá	2	-lúndá	2	-yàgá	1
		-émérá	1					-ràgìrà	1
1	Hippo	-vúbú	10	-bírí	3	-sèrè	3	-jìsìŋgó	2
		-mbémbwà	1					-gùgú	1
1	Housefly	-sówérá	12	-síiyé	2	-sámí	2	-sáázì	1
		-àngí	1	-súcì	1	-zí	1		
1	Ill (to be)	-lwálá	19	-hímbá	1	-sùná	2	-búúká	2
1	Jump (to)	-gúrúká	9	-túúmá	6				
1	Kill (to)	-ttá	19	-lá	1			-hárárà	2

Number out of the 20 Bantu languages having a form similar to each of the cited stems

Use	Meaning		-hùmbó 4	-rú 4	-zwi 2	-sɨgámó 2
1	Knee	-jù 6; -vvìfvì 2	-hùmbó 4	-rú 4	-zwi 2	-sɨgámó 2
1	Leg	-gùlù 15	-gèré 4	-ìgú 1		
1	Lick (to)	-kômbá 13	-rìgasyá 4	-dìyá 1	-rámbá 1	-lùmzì 1
1	Lion	-tálé 8	-pólógómá 7	-tálányì 3	-cúncù 2	
1	Lip	-mwáá 18	-sáyá 1	-bùgwá 1		
4	Man (vs. animal)	-ntú 19	-twákánzì 1	-ròkó 1		
3	Man (vs. woman)	-sájjà 16	-gábò 1	-itó 1	-dùlù 1	-góngò 1
1	Market	-tálé 17	-sókòònì 1		-máná 1	-ènà 1
1	Meat	-nyámá 20	-bèèrè 5	-tààyɩ 2	-tìfti 1	
1	Milk	-tá 12	-sòngì 1			
4	Moon	-èèzì 19	-bù 5	-sùnà 4	-nyènyé 2	-taṇátá 2
1	Mosquito	-sìrì 6	-sìnyá 1	-gùlù 1	-mámbà 1	
1	Mountain	-kúndì 1; -sózì 13; -twá 1	-kùngú 2; -sáwù 1	-sáábù 3		
1	Mud (on a road)	-ītòsì 6; -tómbì 1	-òndò 5		-dòdò 3	
1	Neck	-kótó 11	-syá 7	sîngó 2		
4	New	-ggyá 20				
1	Night	-kírò 18	-jórò 2; -úùlù			
1	Nose	-nyíndo 12				
2	Oil	(Bantu data incomplete)	-púnú 8	-gúrùbè 1	-gòòyá 1	-bérégè 1
1	Pig	-bízzì 9	-fúlá 5	-kéndì 2	-àd+í 1	-kúbà 1
1	Rain	-júrá 10; -dàgálí 1		-hámà 1		
1	Root	-zí 16	-lándírá 2	-rìgitá 2	-kóló 1	-tèètyá 1
2	Run (to)	-irúká 14	-dìmá 2		-dùlúmá 1	
	Salt	(Bantu data incomplete)				
1	See (to)	-bóná 11	-réébá 4	-róra 3	-lábá 1	-zìlbà 1
1	Sell (to)	-túndá 11	-gùlìsá 3	-kùsá 3	-ghùlyá 2	-sòmbéésà 1
4	Sheep	-táámá 41	-kyesè 2	-kòndì 2	-dìgá 1	-bùlì 1
4	Shield	-gábò 20				
4	Shoulder	-bégà 71	-tugù 2	-túùrì 1		

Number out of the 20 Bantu languages having a form similar to each of the cited stems

Use	Meaning					
		(Bantu data incomplete)				
2	Skin	-ggúlù 14	-fúmbi 2	-rèrí 1	-hû 1	-kôbà 1
1	Sky	-búla 1				
1	Snake	-jòkà 12	-sótà 3	-tèmú 3	-pìrì 2	
4	Spear	-ffúmù 17	-símô 1	-tîmù 1	-kòngá 1	-àndá 1
1	Spit (to)	-cwà 7	-fújjá 6	-cwéérá 4	-kyèbá 2	
1	Steal (to)	-bbá 20				
4	Sun	-júbà 14	-sáná 3	-nyààtsá 2	-màní 1	
1	Swallow	-mírá 20				
2	Tail	-kírá 16	-kyìngá 2	-rìzò 1	-kwàngà 1	
		(Bantu data incomplete)				
1	Tongue	-inó 20	-sáàlà 9			
1	Tooth	-tí 11				
1	Tree	-tánáká 8				
1	Vomit (to)	-génda 10	-sésémá 7	-lusá 3	-ròòká 1	-sála 1
1	Walk (to)	-síkà 8	-támbula 5	-ribátá 3	-dètáàga 1	-rùbátángà 1
1	Wall	-tèèpé 1	-séngé 6	-dìní 2	-sídá 2	-pìndí 1
1	Wash (to)	-náába 11	-ógà 6	-sínga 2	-gìsá 1	
4	Water	-zzi 18	-bô 1	-ghétsè 1		
1	Wind	-yàgá 9	-péwò 7	-púngà 2	-bóyò 1	-wèwè 1
4	Wing	-wàwà 20				
4	Woman	-kázi 19	-gólè 1			

compared; and they were always compared segment by segment. In general one stem was classified as being in the same group as another if no segment in it differed from the corresponding segment in another stem by more than two points on a phonetic scale which will be described in detail later. The form of the stem was taken to be that which occurred in the word as given, although there are sometimes grammatical reasons why this may not be the correct approach. Thus in Rutooro the word for 'pig' is **empunu**, and the stem is taken to be **-punu**; but all the derived forms such as **akahunu** (piglet) indicate that the underlying stem is really **-hunu**, and that it changes to **-punu** only when it is preceded by a nasal.

TABLE 2.5: *The word for 'pig' in 20 Ugandan Bantu languages.*

Language	Prefix	Stem					
		C	V	C	V	C	V
Luganda	èm	b	î	zz	í		
Lusoga	ém	b	ìì	dh	í		
Lugwere	óm	b	ì	zz	í		
Lunyole	ém	b	ìì	j	ì		
Lugwe	ém	b	í	c	ì		
Lusamia	ém	b	îì	c	í		
Lukenyi	`m	b	ì	x	í		
Lumasaba (N)	ím	b	ìì	z	í		
Lumasaba (S)	ím	b	ìì	ts	í		
Runyoro	èm	p	ú	n	ù		
Rutooro	èm	p	ù	n	ù		
Ruhororo	èm	p	ù	n	ù		
Runyankore	èm	p	ú	n	ù		
Rukiga	èm	p	ú	n	ú		
Rugungu	`m	p	ú	n	ù		
Rukonjo	`m	b	ú	n	ù		
Lubwisi	èm	p	ù	n	ú		
Ruruli	`m	b	é	r	é	g	è
Runyarwanda	`ŋ	g	ú	r	ú	b	è
Rwamba	`ŋ	g	òò	y	á		

Examination of Table 2.4 will show several cases where different stems have been noted, although the forms are probably historically related. Thus four different stems are shown for 'elephant' although at least the first two (**-jovu, -jojo**) and perhaps also the third (**-zogi**) are variants of the same form in the earlier language from which all these languages are descended. They were noted as separate stems because in this section, where we are not concerned with historical relations, they were sufficiently distinct by our criteria to be regarded as useful discriminators among these languages.

61

Table 2.4 may also show some cases where a wrong division between stem and prefix has been made. But none of these cases are of the kind that would affect the classification of stems as same or different. It would have been appropriate to have made a separate comparison of the prefixes in each word in each language. But unfortunately we did not know enough about many of the languages to be able to do this. There were a number of occasions when it was clear that a word was in the **ki-** class in one group of languages and the **n-** class in another. But without knowing the complete set of possibilities which occur within a language it was sometimes difficult to be sure of the noun class of each word.

Comparisons of the Northern languages were also hampered by our lack of knowledge. There is no doubt that someone familiar with these groups of languages would be better able to separate the stems from the affixes, and would probably find a number of similar stems which we overlooked. On the whole we took a cautious attitude, and did not declare two stems to be similar unless we were fairly sure that we were making a valid comparison. But all our detailed statements concerning the degree of similarity of Northern languages should be treated with reserve.

Mass comparisons of this kind involve an enormous amount of work; but fortunately much of it can be done on a computer. Taking 20 languages and comparing each of them with each of the others required 190 comparisons. For a word list of 100 items this has to be done for each word, and the results of each comparison for each word have to be added together. The work to be reported below involved comparisons of more than 70,000 pairs of words. Arranging the words in each set as in Table 2.5 has to be done by a linguist. But when given this information in the form of numbers, a computer can compare all the possible pairs of words and make the appropriate sums and tabulations.

PHONETIC SIMILARITY

In addition to the 11 words listed in Table 2.4 which were almost identical in the 20 Bantu languages, a further 30 words were very similar in at least 16 languages. When using the technique of counting the number of stems in common, these two groups of words (totalling more than 40 per cent of the list) told us nothing about the relative similarities and differences within this group of

16 languages. (But they did, of course, tell us that they were all very similar.) However, even when a group of stems can be seen to be all related forms, there are often small differences from language to language, as may be seen by looking at the groups of words in Table 2.5. These small differences in pronunciation may be measured in terms of a phonetic scale which specifies the degree of difference between each segment.

The phonetic scale derives from the fact that every sound can be described in terms of the presence or absence of a number of phonetic properties. Each consonant segment in a Ugandan Bantu language can be described as being, or not being: (1) a stop; (2) a nasal; (3) a fricative; (4) anterior—made in the front of the mouth; (5) alveolar—made near the teeth ridge; (6) coronal—made in the centre of the mouth; (7) voiced; (8) long; (9) followed by a w-glide; (10) followed by a y-glide. A partial characterization of some consonants in these terms is given in Tables 2.6 and 2.7. A plus sign indicates the presence of a feature, and a minus sign shows its absence.

TABLE 2.6: *The classification of the places of articulation required for the description of Ugandan Bantu languages.*

| Example | Phonetic term | Characteristic Features | | |
		anterior	alveolar	coronal
b	labial	+	−	−
d+	dental	+	−	+
d	alveolar	+	+	+
d−	postalveolar	−	+	+
j	palatal	−	−	+
g	velar	−	−	−

TABLE 2.7: *The classification of some manners of articulation required for the description of Ugandan Bantu languages.*

| Example | Phonetic term | Characteristic Features | | |
		nasal	stop	fricative
n	nasal	+	−	−
nz	nasal compound fricative	+	−	+
nd	nasal compound stop	+	+	−
d	stop	−	+	−
j	affricate	−	+	+
z	fricative	−	−	+
l/r	approximant	−	−	−

The degree of similarity between segments is taken to be the number of features they have in common. Examples of this measure are shown in Table 2.8. Thus **b** and **d+** (the Lusoga **dh** which is made with the tongue against the teeth) have nine out of the ten

63

points in common; and **b** and **shy** differ in seven points, and have only three points in common.

TABLE 2.8:   *The degree of similarity between some consonant segments in Ugandan Bantu languages.*

	d+	d	d−	j	g	dy	dw	dd	dz	z	nz	l	r	h	s	sh	sy	shy
b	9	8	7	7	9	7	7	7	7	6	5	7	6	7	5	4	4	3
d+		9	8	8	8	8	8	8	8	7	6	8	7	6	6	5	5	4
d			9	7	7	9	9	9	9	8	7	9	8	5	7	6	6	5
d−				8	8	8	8	8	8	7	6	8	9	6	6	7	5	6
j					8	6	6	6	8	7	6	6	7	6	6	7	5	6
g						6	6	6	5	4	6	7	8	4	5	3	4	
dy							8	8	8	7	6	8	7	4	6	5	7	6
dw								8	8	7	6	8	7	4	6	5	5	4
dd									8	7	6	8	7	4	6	5	5	4
dz										9	8	8	7	4	8	7	7	6
z											9	9	8	5	9	8	8	7
nz												8	7	4	8	7	7	6
l													9	6	8	7	7	6
r														7	7	8	6	7
h															6	7	5	6
s																9	9	8
sh																	8	9
sy																		9

In one or two details this measure is not entirely satisfactory.* There is no reason why **b** should be considered to have seven points in common with **l** and only six points in common with **r**. What is more important, there is no reason why **h** should have such varying degrees of similarity with **b**, **d+**, **d**, **d−**. These differences occur because the simple form of classification system used did not allow a feature difference to be considered irrelevant. It was impossible to give a specification of **h** in which it was *equally* different from all these consonants, since the classification system also had to arrange for these consonants to differ from one another. But these inequities probably do not have a significant effect. Among the 8,480 segments compared, **h** occurred only 31 times.

In specifying the vowels we have to consider whether each is, or is not: (1) high; (2) mid; (3) low; (4) front; (5) central; (6) back; (7) long; (8) high tone; (9) falling tone. At one time we added the possibility: (10) low tone. But preliminary results showed that this gave too much importance to tonal similarity, and it is better to consider low tone as simply the absence of high or falling tone. The degree of similarity in vowels is measured by counting the

*More sophisticated measures of phonetic similarity are considered in Ladefoged (1970).

number of features they have in common, in the same way as for consonants.

Using this measure of the degree of phonetic similarity, the features in each segment were compared with the corresponding features in the corresponding segment in each of 30 words in the 20 Bantu languages given in Table 2.5. The 30 words chosen were those which had the same form in at least 16 of the 20 languages. The 228,000 comparisons involved, the sums indicating the degree of phonetic similarity of each pair of languages, and the tabulations were all done on a computer. Only stems were compared, and they were all considered to consist of alternating sequences of vowels and consonants.

MUTUAL INTELLIGIBILITY

We tested the extent to which two different groups of people (the Baganda and the Banyankole) could understand languages related to their own. In each case the test consisted of playing recordings of stories to children in the top class of primary school. We did not record the ages of the children in these classes, but in work in similar classes reported in Part 3, we found that the average age was 13.5. This is around the ideal age for this kind of test. We wanted listeners who would answer on the basis of their knowledge of their own language and who had not been exposed to other Ugandan languages, and who were able to take objective tests. School children were the most suitable group available. As will be reported at a future date, we found it almost impossible to get adults in rural areas to do multiple choice tests. But primary school children are used to this sort of thing; and they are also available in convenient size groups for testing.

Before the children took the test (and even before they knew what it was about) they were assisted in completing a form which asked about the languages they had learnt or been exposed to, and the languages which they thought they could understand. (After the test they realized that they could understand far more than they thought they could.) Everyone in the class took the test, but we discarded the papers of anyone who had been exposed to a second Ugandan language by virtue of its being spoken in his family, or by having lived for some time in another language area.

There were eight stories in the test, each being about 50 words long and having three or four sentences. The stories were of the kind that might have been short news items on the radio. After each story the listeners were asked what it was about, and were presented with three possible answers. The story was then played to them again, and the possible answers also presented again, this time with a request to mark the correct number on the answer sheet. The possible answers were all written in full on the answer sheets, as well as being given on the tape recording. Everything else, including all the standardized instructions, were given only on the tape recording.

All the instructions, all the answers, and the first three stories were in English, using a controlled vocabulary which was known to be well within the understanding of children in the top class in primary school. The first three stories were regarded simply as practice material. The remaining five stories were each in a different language.

We might have just played a different story in each language to one group of listeners. But then, if they had got more correct answers for one story than for another, we would not have known if that was because the questions about that story were easier, or because the listening group found that language easier to understand. Accordingly tests were conducted in five different schools in each area. If we consider the five stories after the practice material to be numbered 1, 2, 3, 4, 5, and the five languages to be denoted by the letters A, B, C, D, E, then the first listening group heard story 1 in language A, story 2 in language B, etc., but the second group heard story 1 in language B, story 2 in language C, etc. The complete arrangement of the material heard by each of the five listening groups was as shown in Table 2.9.

TABLE 2.9: *Relation between listening groups, test stories, and languages A, B, C, D, E.*

		Stories				
		1	2	3	4	5
Listening Groups	1	A	B	C	D	E
	2	B	C	D	E	A
	3	C	D	E	A	B
	4	D	E	A	B	C
	5	E	A	B	C	D

It may be seen that each story occurs once in each language and once in each listening group; and each listening group hears each story once and each language once. We can therefore calculate the average ability of each listening group (the average of each row), the average difficulty of each story (the average of each column), and the average difficulty of each language (the average of each letter). Statistical techniques will show if any of these three groups of averages contain significant variations.

In the general discussion of the similarities and differences between languages we will be considering simply the relative degree of comprehension of various languages, without discussing further how these figures were calculated. Accordingly, so that the data might be available, the actual results of the tests are given here in Tables 2.10a and b. The score associated with the occurrence of a story in a given language was the percentage of the listening group getting the answer correct. A statistical treatment (analysis of

TABLE 2.10a: *Scores for five groups of Luganda speakers listening to their own and four other languages. The five stories were rotated as shown in Table 2.9.*

LANGUAGES

Group size	Luganda	Rutooro	Runyankore	Lusoga	Lumasaba	Group mean
13	92	32	32	61	54	54
20	95	45	55	75	75	69
69	69	52	45	55	35	51
37	92	70	51	54	24	58
31	81	45	87	87	42	68
Language mean	86	49	54	66	46	
Relative comprehension	100	30	40	62	25	

TABLE 2.10b: *Scores for five groups of Runyankore speakers listening to their own and four other languages. The five stories were rotated as shown in Table 2.9.*

LANGUAGES

Group size	Luganda	Rutooro	Runyankore	Rukiga	Lumasaba	Group mean
9	89	78	100	100	22	78
18	78	92	92	83	55	80
13	94	77	85	85	15	71
29	83	76	66	62	24	62
26	27	65	96	77	15	56
Language mean	74	78	88	81	24	
Relative comprehension	75	82	100	87	0	

variance) showed that there was no significant difference between the average scores of any of the listening groups, or between the average scores of any of the stories. But there were always significant differences in the comprehension of the different languages.

Since the task was to choose the correct one out of three possible answers, a group of listeners who had no knowledge of any of the languages might get about one third of the answers correct simply by chance. When less than a third of a listening group got the correct answer, we can say that there was no comprehension of this language. The maximum that can be expected of a group listening to a language other than their own is that they should do as well as they do on their own language. We have considered the relative degree of comprehension of a language to be the proportion of correct answers above the chance level relative to the number of correct answers above the chance level which occurs when the group listens to its own language. Accordingly, when we say that for Luganda speakers the relative degree of comprehension of Lusoga is 62 per cent, we mean that the number of Luganda speaking primary school children who got the correct answer is 62 per cent of the way between the number that would have been expected on a chance basis, and the number who got the correct answer when listening to Luganda.

THE BANTU LANGUAGES

The Ugandan Bantu languages may be considered first of all in terms of an Eastern and a Western group. To a great extent the degree of similarity among the languages within each group is directly related to the geographical distance between them. In nearly every case, each language is most like the languages around it; and the further one goes in any direction, the more the languages begin to differ. Because there is often a relationship between a language and those all around it in the same group, it is difficult to list all the languages in a satisfactory order. This is evident in the presentation of our results in Table 2.11, which shows the word list comparisons for 20 Ugandan Bantu languages. In a table of this kind each language has to be placed between only two others; but in fact it may be equally similar to several others.

Figure 2.7 is a better way of representing the relationship between the languages which can be fitted into the two main groups. In this figure the distance between any two languages is roughly proportional to their degree of similarity. Of course, since each language can vary independently of all the others, it is impossible to make the distances between each of them exactly correct when more than three languages have to be plotted on a two dimensional chart. But the degree of error in Figure 2.7 is not great enough to affect their relative positions (the rank order of similarity between each of them and each of the others).

It may be seen that the Eastern languages are all fairly distinct from one another, with the exception of Lusamia and Lugwe, which are usually considered to be dialects of the same language. The next closest pair among the Eastern languages is Luganda and Lusoga. Many of the Western languages are much closer to one another. On our figures, Runyoro and Rutooro are slightly closer to one another than Lusamia and Lugwe. They are often referred to as if they were a single language. Runyankore and Rukiga are equally close; and they are also frequently treated as if they were one. In fact six of the Western languages, Runyankore, Rukiga, Runyoro, Rutooro and Rutagwenda are all so similar that they might be regarded simply as dialects of the one language (which might, following a suggestion made to us by Mr. Mosha, be called Rutara, since it is in the area of the former Kitara Kingdom). If we choose to consider all these languages to be merely dialects in this way, we should, if we keep to the same scale of similarity, consider Luganda, Lusoga and Lukenyi to be merely different dialects of one language. Several of the Western languages are spoken by people who were not separately enumerated in the 1959 census. The speakers of Ruhororo were probably included in with those of Runyankore or Rukiga, since not only are the languages very similar, but also the old kingdom of Mpororo is between Ankole and Kigezi. Rutagwenda, which is linguistically and geographically between Runyoro/Rutooro and Runyankore/Rukiga, is spoken by another group who were not separately enumerated in the 1959 census. The same is true of Rugungu, which is spoken near the shores of Lake Albert in the North of Bunyoro, and Lubwisi, which is spoken on the North Western side of the Ruwenzori mountains.

It is very interesting that it is possible to show these relationships so adequately on charts as in Figure 2.7; and that the relative positions of the languages are fairly similar to their positions on

69

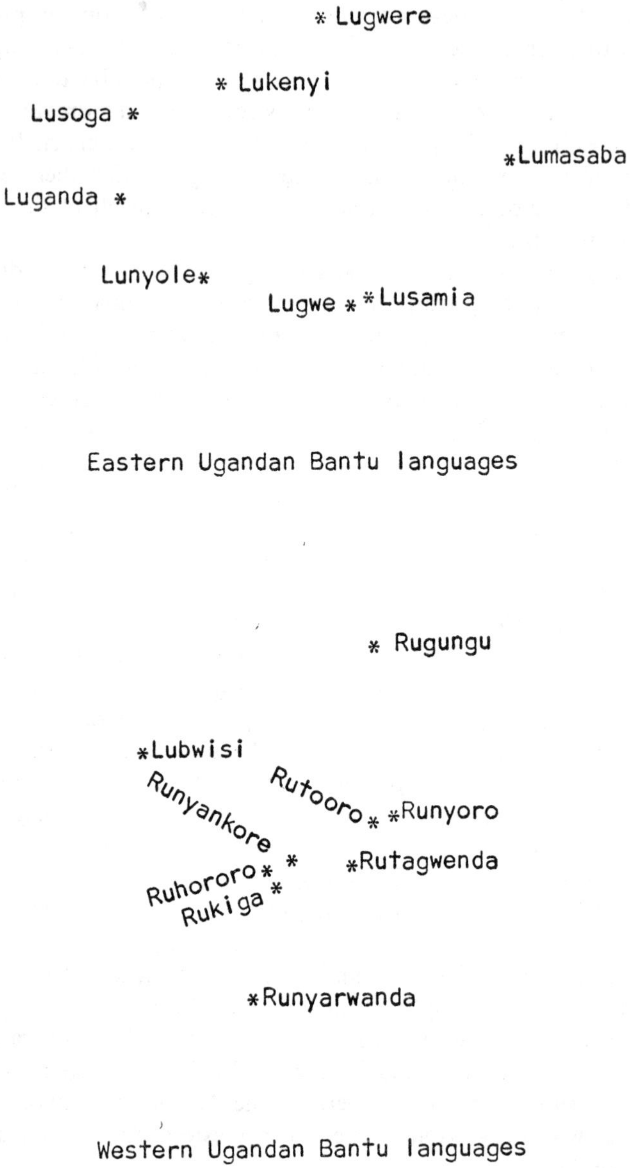

* Lugwere

* Lukenyi

Lusoga *

*Lumasaba

Luganda *

Lunyole*

Lugwe **Lusamia

Eastern Ugandan Bantu languages

* Rugungu

*Lubwisi

Runyankore

Rutooro * *Runyoro

Ruhororo* *

Rukiga *

*Rutagwenda

*Runyarwanda

Western Ugandan Bantu languages

Figure 2.7: *The Eastern and Western Ugandan Bantu languages arranged so that the distance between them corresponds to the degree of similarity in word lists. Note that Rwamba, Rukonjo and Ruruli cannot be represented in either section.*

70

TABLE 2.11: *Percent words in common among Ugandan Bantu languages.*

	Lumasaba	Lunyole	Lusamia	Lugwe	Lugwere	Lukenyi	Lusoga	Luganda	Ruruli	Runyoro	Rutooro	Ruhororo	Rutagwenda	Runyankore	Rukiga	Lubwisi	Runyarwanda	Rukonjo	Rugungu	Rwamba	Mean
Lumasaba	—	54	70	74	74	64	55	54	49	48	50	49	49	49	49	44	46	38	34	21	51
Lunyole	54	—	80	82	64	76	70	66	58	55	59	56	55	56	56	50	49	44	51	22	58
Lusamia	70	80	—	92	60	62	64	61	52	54	56	55	55	57	55	47	50	44	45	22	56
Lugwe	74	82	92	—	60	63	65	62	56	54	56	55	55	57	55	48	49	45	48	22	58
Lugwere	74	64	60	60	—	76	70	66	66	56	56	54	54	51	55	49	47	49	54	23	57
Lukenyi	64	76	62	63	76	—	81	74	66	61	60	60	59	57	61	51	48	49	55	23	60
Lusoga	55	70	64	65	70	81	—	86	65	68	64	66	64	64	67	56	53	53	55	27	63
Luganda	54	66	61	62	66	74	86	—	62	65	64	66	63	63	68	54	50	51	54	24	61
Ruruli	49	58	52	56	66	66	65	62	—	71	69	67	67	65	58	58	54	54	60	31	59
Runyoro	48	55	54	54	56	61	68	65	71	—	93	86	90	86	87	72	62	64	64	33	67
Rutooro	50	59	56	56	56	60	64	64	69	93	—	84	91	86	85	73	63	63	65	32	66
Ruhororo	49	56	55	55	54	60	66	66	67	86	84	—	91	96	96	67	60	64	56	30	66
Rutagwenda	49	55	55	55	54	59	64	63	67	90	91	91	—	93	90	70	65	62	60	31	66
Runyankore	49	56	57	57	51	57	64	63	65	86	86	96	93	—	94	68	64	63	54	30	67
Rukiga	49	56	55	55	55	61	67	68	58	87	85	96	90	94	—	68	55	57	59	31	66
Lubwisi	44	50	47	48	49	51	56	54	58	72	73	67	70	68	68	—	55	64	49	31	57
Runyarwanda	46	49	50	49	47	48	53	50	54	62	63	60	65	64	55	55	—	64	54	38	57
Rukonjo	38	44	44	45	49	49	53	51	54	64	63	64	62	63	57	64	64	—	52	34	53
Rugungu	34	51	45	48	54	55	55	54	60	64	65	56	60	54	59	49	54	52	—	29	53
Rwamba	21	22	22	22	23	23	27	24	31	33	32	30	31	30	31	31	38	34	29	—	28

F

Map 1. Neither of these facts is necessarily true of the relationships within sets of languages. They might have been impossible to represent on two dimensional charts without distorting their relative similarity; or it might have been possible to represent them in this way, but with little or no resemblance to the present geographical location of their speakers. From the results we have obtained (and especially if the same relationships can be substantiated with the more rigorous techniques of historical linguistics) we might infer that each of the two groups had a single parent language, the speakers of which became more and more dispersed geographically and more and more distinct linguistically. Alternatively, as a slightly different hypothesis, we might still conclude that the two groups had different origins, but that the present relationships are due to the degree of contact between speakers of the different languages in the past.

Some previously published linguistic comparisons suggest a different grouping of the Ugandan Bantu languages. Most of the languages shown in both parts of Figure 2.7 together with Kirundi and some other languages, have all been put into a single group called Interlacustrine Bantu. But in this grouping some of the languages that we have put in the Eastern Ugandan Bantu group have been left out. Thus the various dialects of Lumasaba are put in a group which is not considered to be part of Interlacustrine Bantu; and Lunyole, Lusamia and Lugwe are also said to be in another group, together with the Luhya languages of Kenya. There is no doubt that Lusamia and Lugwe are very like the languages just across the border. But they, and Lunyole, are not in a group which is clearly distinct from the other Eastern Ugandan Bantu languages.

It is actually not altogether clear that there are two distinct groups within Uganda. It is true that without slightly distorting the relative degrees of similarity of the languages within each group it is impossible to take any of the Eastern languages and put them in with the Western languages, or to take any of the Western languages and put them in with the Eastern languages. But despite this apparent distinction between the two groups, it is also true that Luganda, the Westernmost member of the Eastern group, is the most similar to the Western languages. To some extent it might be possible to regard all the languages in Figure 2.7 as part of a continuum stretching over much of Uganda, and (adding the Luhya languages) going on into Kenya.

There are, however, a number of Ugandan Bantu languages which do not fit easily on either part of Figure 2.7. Among them are two languages, Rukonjo and Rwamba, which cannot be easily associated with any of the languages previously mentioned in this section, or with each other. We saw in the section on sound systems that these two were also distinguished by being the only Ugandan Bantu languages with seven contrasting vowels. Of the two, Rukonjo is the most like the Western Ugandan Bantu languages. It is spoken all over the Ruwenzori mountains. Rwamba is spoken in the part of Uganda to the West of these mountains, and in neighbouring parts of the Congo. As can be seen from Table 2.11, it is the most distinct of all the Ugandan Bantu languages. Speakers of Rwamba and Lubwisi seem to have been counted together in the 1959 census, although these languages are very different from each other. It is difficult to say how many speakers there are of each, but our impression is that in the neighbourhood of Bundibugyo there may be about equal numbers.

Table 2.11 also includes data on Ruruli, which is spoken in the North of Buganda and the South East of Bunyoro. Many of the speakers of this language refer to themselves as Baganda or Banyoro (and probably all of them were counted as such in the 1959 census). Linguistically they are a distinct group, with only a slightly higher affinity to the Western than to the Eastern group.

In addition to the data on the languages discussed above, we also have some supplementary data in the form of word lists collected by student fieldworkers. Some of this material is summarized in Table 2.12. The first three languages, Lulamogi, Lusiki, and Ludiope, are all spoken in Busoga. The first two are linguistically and geographically between Lusoga and Lugwere; and the third is most like Lusoga, but with greater similarity to Luganda than to Lugwere. The next two languages, Luvuma and Lusese, are spoken in two of the groups of islands in Lake Victoria which became part of the Kingdom of Buganda towards the end of the last century. Luvuma is (linguistically and geographically) very close to both Lusoga and Luganda; but Lusese appears to be much more similar to the Western languages, Runyankore and Rutooro, perhaps because of relationships prior to its incorporation in Buganda. Unfortunately we do not have any data on Lukome, which is the language spoken in the third major group of islands in the North of Lake Victoria. Most people on all three of these groups of islands report that they

73

are bilingual, being able to speak Luganda as well as their own island language. It would seem that these smaller languages will not be spoken much longer.

Table 2.12 also shows data on Lunabuddu, Lukooki, and Lunaziba, all of which are spoken (usually only by older people) in the South of Buganda, but which are nevertheless far more akin to Runyankore. These languages are said to be very similar to Kihaya which is spoken in the adjacent part of Tanzania. Lastly, it may be seen that Runyara, which is spoken in the North East of Buganda, is not very similar to either the Eastern or the Western languages, but is very like Ruruli.

TABLE 2.12: *Percent words in common between some of the listed Bantu languages and some additional languages and dialects.*

	Lugwere	Lusoga	Luganda	Runyankore	Rutooro	Ruruli
Lulamogi	79	79	73	56	57	67
Lusiki	81	81	75	60	61	61
Ludiope	74	91	85	64	65	70
Luvuma	70	89	88	65	67	70
Lusese	59	68	66	81	80	71
Lunabuddu	59	70	69	87	82	71
Lukooki	60	72	71	89	83	73
Lunaziba	54	63	59	85	84	71
Runyara	73	71	69	66	71	91

At this point it is worth considering some of our other data on the relations between these languages, so that we can appreciate what it means to say that they have a certain percentage of their words in common. We conducted comprehension tests among two groups speaking Bantu languages. Table 2.13 shows the results.

TABLE 2.13: *Comprehension scores for speakers of Luganda and Runyankore.*

First language of listening group	Languages used in the test and % comprehension relative to first language of listening group			
Luganda	Lusoga	Runyankore	Rutooro	Lumasaba
	62	40	30	25
Runyankore	Rukiga	Rutooro	Luganda	Lumasaba
	87	82	75	0

In general the degree of comprehension is in very good accord with the word list relationships that have been described above. Speakers of Luganda can understand Lusoga best of the four languages on which they were tested, and Lumasaba worst. Speakers of Runyankore can understand nearly everything that is said in Rukiga, but can only guess at the meaning of anything in Lumasaba.

It is interesting to see the extent to which the degree of mutual intelligibility of two languages can be predicted from knowing the percentage of words they have in common. Table 2.13 showed the degree of one way comprehension of eight pairs of languages, Luganda to four others, and Runyankore to four others (counting Luganda to Runyankore as a different pair from Runyankore to Luganda). Table 2.11 included the percentage of words in common for all these pairs (but in this case the percentage of words in common between Luganda and Runyankore is of course the same as that between Runyankore and Luganda). The relationship between these two measures of similarity between languages is shown in Figure 2.8. The crosses represent data for the Runyankore based pairs, and the circles for the Luganda based pairs. Thus the lowest cross represents the fact that Runyankore has 49 per cent words in common with Lumasaba, and the fact that speakers of Runyankore could not understand Lumasaba at all. The double point at 100 per cent indicates the independent data, given by our definitions, that both groups could understand their own languages with maximum comprehension. We could have plotted the five actual test scores for each of the two groups of listeners, instead of reducing these scores to the four relative comprehension scores. Then it would have been more obvious that there were ten independent pairs of numbers. We did not do it this way because the actual test scores are on an arbitrary scale.

If we neglect for the moment one point which is separate from the rest, we can say that there is a very high correlation between the percentage of words in common and the degree of comprehension. On the basis of the other nine points we can calculate the position of a line (the solid line in the figure) which allows us to make the best possible predictions of the degree of comprehension from a knowledge of the number of words in common. This line shows that if two languages have 72 per cent of their words in common there will probably be about 50 per cent comprehension. We can also tell how accurate our predictions might be. The dashed lines on either side of the solid line indicate the probable range of error. There is, statistically, less than one chance in 20 that our predictions might be wrong by a greater amount than this. So if two languages have 72 per cent of their words in common we can be reasonably sure that there will be more than 40 per cent and less than 60 per cent comprehension.

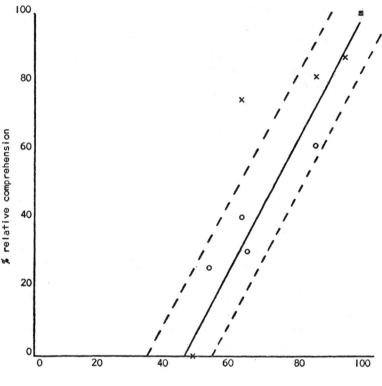

Figure 2.8: *The relation between the percentage of words in common and the degree of comprehension, relative to the first language.*

There are, however, circumstances in which our predictions would be wrong. These are exemplified by the point which lies well outside the dashed lines. This point represents the number of words in common between Luganda and Runyankore, in comparison with the amount of Luganda that Runyankore speakers can understand. Apparently they understand far more Luganda than would have been predicted. This is probably because Luganda is very widely spoken and has been a language with a high prestige. It is spoken in the capital of the country, and has more time on the radio than any other Ugandan language. All the Runyankore listening group claimed that they were monolinguals and could not understand Luganda. But nevertheless they have been constantly exposed to it on the radio and elsewhere; and they could in fact understand it quite well.

We may conclude that within this group of languages, knowledge of the percentage of words in common allows us to predict the degree of comprehension, except when questions of prestige are involved. This effect may work in two ways, although we have a clear cut indication of only one in our figures. It is quite possible that in some circumstances speakers of one language may do worse in understanding another than expected, because they do not consider it to have as much prestige as their language.

It was impossible to test the degree of comprehension of all the pairs of languages because of the labour involved. Finding out the comprehension of each of the languages in Table 2.11 relative to all the others would involve at least 190 lengthy test sessions, each with a different set of recordings. Accordingly the major part of the comparisons between languages must be mainly in terms of the percentage of words in common.

Finally, we must consider data on the extent to which these languages sound alike. The degree of phonetic similarity between some of the Ugandan Bantu languages is shown in Table 2.14. The languages listed in this table are the same as those in Table 2.11, except that two different forms of Lumasaba have been noted, and Rutagwenda has been left out. The scale is arbitrary, and has been made to be of the same order of magnitude as in the word list comparisons. It may be seen that in general the same relationships hold: each language is most similar to the languages around it. But this measure provides less differentiation among the more distant languages.

There is no inevitable reason why the degree of phonetic similarity between members of a group of languages should be similar to the percentages of words they have in common. But because these measures go together it is not surprising that they are good indicators of mutual intelligibility.

THE CENTRAL SUDANIC LANGUAGES

There are usually said to be two Sudanic languages spoken in Uganda, Lugbara and Madi, each with several different dialects.

77

TABLE 2.14: The degree of phonetic similarity between some Ugandan Bantu languages.

	Lumasaba (S)	Lumasaba (N)	Lunyole	Lusamia	Lugwe	Lugwere	Lukenyi	Lusoga	Luganda	Ruruli	Runyoro	Rutooro	Ruhororo	Runyankore	Rukiga	Lubwisi	Runyarwanda	Rukonjo	Rugungu	Rwamba	Mean
Lumasaba (S)	—	85	76	78	81	73	79	76	74	73	71	77	72	77	73	69	68	69	60	47	73
Lumasaba (N)	85	—	82	80	80	78	83	81	79	74	77	80	77	82	83	71	75	68	68	52	76
Lunyole	76	82	—	88	87	76	81	85	80	71	73	77	70	73	75	67	73	65	63	46	74
Lusamia	78	80	88	—	97	75	80	83	80	71	72	75	71	71	76	67	73	65	62	48	74
Lugwe	81	80	87	97	—	74	82	81	79	71	72	75	72	74	77	68	75	66	62	48	75
Lugwere	73	78	76	75	74	—	81	75	75	80	73	76	71	77	74	70	71	65	63	48	72
Lukenyi	79	83	81	80	82	81	—	85	84	78	79	82	77	81	83	74	75	70	67	50	77
Lusoga	76	81	85	83	81	75	85	—	82	75	74	77	74	78	77	71	74	68	65	50	75
Luganda	74	79	80	80	79	75	84	82	—	72	80	82	78	78	81	70	65	67	61	46	74
Ruruli	73	74	71	71	71	80	78	75	72	—	77	76	71	77	71	74	66	67	65	52	72
Runyoro	71	77	73	72	72	73	79	74	80	77	—	93	87	88	86	76	75	70	70	46	76
Rutooro	77	80	77	75	75	76	82	77	82	76	93	—	88	90	88	77	76	71	67	47	77
Ruhororo	72	77	70	71	72	71	77	74	78	71	87	88	—	90	87	70	75	71	64	46	74
Runyankore	77	82	73	71	74	77	81	78	78	77	88	90	90	—	86	77	75	74	66	52	77
Rukiga	73	83	75	76	77	74	83	77	81	71	86	88	87	86	—	74	80	69	58	50	77
Lubwisi	69	71	67	67	68	70	74	71	70	74	76	77	70	77	74	—	69	66	67	55	70
Runyarwanda	68	75	73	73	75	71	75	74	65	66	75	76	75	75	80	69	—	70	67	48	71
Rukonjo	69	68	65	65	66	65	70	68	67	67	70	71	71	74	69	66	70	—	64	48	67
Rugungu	60	68	63	62	62	63	67	65	61	65	70	67	64	66	58	67	67	64	—	44	63
Rwamba	47	52	46	48	48	48	50	50	46	52	46	47	46	52	50	55	48	48	44	—	48

But there is no linguistic reason why there should be two languages rather than one with a larger number of dialects, or more than two each with a smaller number of dialects. Crazzolara, in his grammar of Lugbara, says 'Lugbara . . . is one of the Ma'di languages. It differs considerably from the Ma'di spoken in the neighbouring north-eastern regions by the Moyo and Opari . . .' But he goes on to say, 'Only a short time, say about a month, is necessary in the neighbouring region to pick up, more or less, the other language without much difficulty.' (Our own observations are that this is an underestimate of the degree of difficulty for the Lugbara who has to learn the Madi of Moyo.)

We have examined what we arbitrarily called three dialects of Lugbara and four dialects of Madi. The relations between these languages are as indicated in Table 2.15. It should be remembered that the percentages shown in the table are almost certainly much lower than they would have been if the comparisons had been made by a native speaker of one of these languages; but the relative degrees of similarity are probably about right. Standard Lugbara, which we take to be that spoken in Arua, is closer to the Terego dialect than to the Aringa dialect; in fact the Aringa dialect appears to be rather different. Standard Lugbara is closer to the Okollo dialect of Madi than it is to the Aringa dialect. There seems to be some form of dialect continuum, with the Aringa dialect of Lugbara being actually closer to the Ogoko dialect of Madi than to either of the other Lugbara dialects.

TABLE 2.15:   *Percent words in common among Central Sudanic languages.*

	Lugbara (Standard)	Lugbara (Terego)	Lugbara (Aringa)	Madi (Okollo)	Madi (Ogoko)	Madi (Moyo)	Madi (Oyuwi)	Kebu	Mean (excluding Kebu)
Lugbara (Standard)	—	80	68	76	67	69	58	10	70
Lugbara (Terego	80	—	71	63	72	67	60	10	69
Lugbara (Aringa)	68	71	—	59	76	66	65	10	68
Madi (Okollo)	76	63	59	—	59	63	52	11	62
Madi (Ogoko)	67	72	76	59	—	67	74	11	69
Madi (Moyo)	69	67	66	63	67	—	75	13	68
Madi (Oyuwi)	58	60	65	52	74	75	—	12	64
Kebu	10	10	10	11	11	13	12	—	—

In addition to Lugbara and Madi, other Sudanic languages are spoken in the same part of Uganda, mainly by people belonging to small groups of tribes which are centred in the Congo. They include Kebu and Lendu. As can be seen from Table 2.15 there is only a very small similarity between the words of Kebu and those of Lugbara and Madi. But it is, of course, greater than the degree of similarity between Kebu and any language belonging to another language family.

WESTERN NILOTIC LANGUAGES

The relations between the Western Nilotic languages are shown in Table 2.16. Some of them are very close to one another. The principal members of the group, Acholi, Alur, and Lango have, by our test, between 84 and 90 per cent of their vocabulary in

TABLE 2.16: *Percent words in common among Western Nilotic languages.*

	Nyakwai	Labwor	Acholi	Dhopaluo	Alur	Lango	Kumam	Dhopadhola	Mean
Nyakwai	—	89	88	89	85	88	80	78	85
Labwor	89	—	90	89	85	91	78	73	85
Acholi	88	90	—	90	89	89	77	76	86
Dhopaluo	89	89	90	—	86	89	82	78	86
Alur	85	85	89	86	—	84	73	74	82
Lango	88	91	89	89	84	—	81	73	85
Kumam	80	78	77	82	73	81	—	68	77
Dhopadhola	78	73	76	78	74	73	68	—	74

common. These are very high figures, especially considering the way in which the test is likely to underestimate the true degree of similarity in the word lists. As we have seen, languages which have about this percentage of words in common are fairly mutually intelligible. Each of these languages has several local variants; with the exception of the Jonam dialect of Alur (which has about 96 per cent of its vocabulary in common with the Alur spoken in Ngora, the neighbouring county) these are not usually considered to be clearly distinguishable. Dhopaluo (or Chopi) the language spoken by the Jopaluo South of the Nile in Bunyoro, and Nyakwai and Labwor, two languages spoken in the North of Karamoja, are also all very similar to Acholi, Alur and Lango, despite the fact that Labwor is sometimes said to belong to the Eastern Nilotic (Nilohamitic) group. Kumam, which is spoken in the West of Teso

District is only slightly more different. The Kumam (like the Langi) may have been of Nilohamitic origin; and Kumam certainly contains a number of words (17 per cent) in common with Ateso, which is undeniably an Eastern Nilotic language. But Kumam is clearly even more akin to the Western Nilotic group. Dhopadhola is the most distinct language in this group. The Jopadhola are now entirely surrounded by Bantu speaking people (who refer to them as the Badama and their language as Ludama). The Ugandan Western Nilotic languages are sometimes referred to collectively as Lwo; but this term is also used in the more specific sense as a cover term for just Acholi and Lango.

EASTERN NILOTIC LANGUAGES

The Eastern Nilotic or Nilohamitic languages are the most diverse group in Uganda. Ateso is the language spoken by the largest number of people in this group. The dialect spoken in Ngora is usually said to be the central or standard form. We also considered two other dialects, one spoken in Bukedi District near Pallisa, and the other spoken near Tororo (which is probably the most conservative form). All three forms turned out to be very similar, with (as shown in Table 2.17) at least 87 per cent of their words in common. The Ateso dialects are also all fairly similar to some of the languages spoken in Karamoja, notably Ngakarimojong, Jie, Ngadotho (spoken by the Dodoth), and Ngapore (spoken by the Poren). These four languages of Karamoja form a compact group with 79–95 per cent of their words in common. Using the figures for the Ateso dialects as a comparison, we might well call at least Jie and Ngadotho simply dialects of Ngakarimojong.

The remaining Eastern Nilotic languages are very different from those we have mentioned so far. Mening, which is spoken in the very North of Karamoja, is the most similar to Ateso and Ngakarimojong, but it is clearly a different language. Tepeth, spoken by a small group (about 5,000 people) on Mount Moroto, is even more distinct. Kakwa, a much larger language, is spoken in the North of West Nile by more than 45,000 people in Uganda and by three times as many more in the Sudan and the Congo. It has only a very small degree of similarity with Ateso or any of the other Eastern Nilotic languages. Kupsabiny, the language spoken by the Sebei, has some likeness to its neighbour, Suk (or Pokot), but is otherwise

81

TABLE 2.17: *Percent words in common among Eastern Nilotic languages.*

	Ateso (Ngora)	Ateso (Pallisa)	Ateso (Tororo)	Ngakarimojong	Jie	Ngadotho	Ngapore	Mening	Tepeth	Kakwa	Kupsabiny (Sebei)	Suk (Pokot)	Ik (Teuso)	Mean
Ateso (Ngora)		90	87	73	73	71	70	22	10	11	10	10	4	44
Ateso (Pallisa)	90		89	73	72	72	69	21	10	14	10	10	4	45
Ateso (Tororo)	87	89		75	75	73	71	22	11	12	10	11	5	46
Ngakarimojong	73	73	75		95	88	79	21	16	13	9	6	6	46
Jie	73	72	75	95		90	83	21	16	12	9	6	7	47
Ngadotho	71	72	73	88	90		80	21	16	10	9	6	7	45
Ngapore	70	69	71	79	83	80		20	15	13	10	6	5	43
Mening	22	21	22	21	21	21	20		8	16	9	7	5	16
Tepeth	10	10	11	16	16	16	15	8		5	4	4	3	10
Kakwa	11	14	12	13	12	10	13	16	5		2	2	3	9
Kupsabiny (Sebei)	10	10	10	9	9	9	10	9	4	2		38	5	10
Suk (Pokot)	10	10	11	6	6	6	7	4	2	2	38		3	9
Ik (Teuso)	4	4	4	6	7	7	5	5	3	3	5	3		5

distinct from any other members of the group. Lastly Ik (or Teuso) spoken by a few thousand people in the North East of Karamoja, is so different that we have no real grounds for putting it into this— or any other—group.

SUMMARY

It might be helpful if we concluded this section with a tabular presentation of the languages and dialects of Uganda. We will take a figure of 75 per cent words in common as the level at or above which we will consider two different speech forms as being merely dialects of one language. In terms of our intelligibility tests this corresponds to slightly more than 50 per cent comprehension, or a little more than half way between the number of correct answers to questions due to chance and the number of correct answers which are given when listening to one's own language. On this basis we find that there are about 30 different languages in Uganda, 12 being Bantu languages, 7 Sudanic, 3 Eastern Nilotic and 8 Western Nilotic. It should be remembered that due to our lack of knowledge of the Sudanic languages, our figures are probably very inaccurate in this area; there are probably really fewer than 7 distinct languages in this group. The complete list of languages and dialects is given in Table 2.18.

TABLE 2.18:   *The distinct languages of Uganda.*

1.   Bantu
1. Lumasaba
2. Lunyole
3. Lusamia, Lugwe
4. Lugwere
5. Luganda, Lusoga, Lukenyi
6. Ruruli
7. Rutara: Runyoro, Rutooro, Ruhororo, Rutagwenda, Runyankore, Rukiga
8. Rukonjo
9. Runyarwanda
10. Lubwisi
11. Rugungu
12. Rwamba

2.   Sudanic
1. Lugbara (Standard), Lugbara (Terego)
2. Lugbara (Aringa)
3. Madi (Okollo)
4. Madi (Ogoko)
5. Madi (Moyo)
6. Madi (Oyuwi)
7. Kebu

TABLE 2.18: *The distinct languages of Uganda (cont.).*

3. *Western Nilotic*
   1. Acholi, Lango, Alur, Dhopaluo, Labwor, Nyakwai
   2. Kumam
   3. Dhopadhola

4. *Eastern Nilotic*
   1. Ateso
   2. Ngakarimojong, Jie, Ngadotho, Ngapore
   3. Mening
   4. Tepeth
   5. Kakwa
   6. Kupsabiny
   7. Suk
   8. Ik

PART 3

Language in Education

INTRODUCTION

The base of the present system of education in Uganda is the seven year primary school. There are 2,648 government aided primary schools enrolling a total of 641,639 children, roughly 50 per cent of the age group. Of the figure, 37.7 per cent are girls but the actual percentage is lower in the upper primary grades. There are 19,257 teachers in the primary schools with an overall pupil-teacher ratio of 33:1.

Primary education is neither free nor compulsory. Fees average about 20 shillings per year for the first two classes, 40 shillings in classes III through VI, and 150 shillings in the final year (Primary VII). Fees are slightly lower for girls in some districts. Although education is not compulsory, there is a demand for more places than the government is able to provide. This gap is filled in some districts by a number of unaided private schools, staffed largely by untrained teachers, which provide additional places for children in Primary I, II and III. Frequently children who have been enrolled in these unaided schools are able to enter government aided schools in Primary IV as places become available due to expansion of facilities or because places are left by children who drop out of school.

There are four types of post-primary institutions. Entrance to these schools is largely dependent on the pupil's ability in English, since all teaching at this level is in English.

The first type of institution is the senior secondary school. This is by far the most prestigious. In 1967 there were 71 grant-aided schools enrolling about 20,000 pupils, about 4,000 of whom were girls. The secondary school provides four years of general education leading to the School Certificate. Seventeen secondary schools offer advanced level work beyond these four years which leads to the Higher School Certificate, the level required for university entrance. In 1966 the total enrolment in Secondary 5 and 6 was 1,545 pupils.

Entrance to secondary school is dependent on total marks earned in English and Mathematics in the Primary Leaving Examination. A further consideration, however, is the ability to pay school fees which range from 450 to 650 shillings per year in boarding schools and 250 to 450 shillings in day schools. A number of government bursaries are available, but the demand far exceeds the supply.

There are a large number of private secondary schools, some of which are licensed and supervised by the Ministry of Education, although they receive no financial support. Standards vary considerably in these schools, but there is always a demand for places.

A second type of post-primary institution is the Grade II teacher training college. There are 26 such schools located throughout the country which provide four years of training. The first two years concentrate on general education, similar in scope to the secondary school, and the last two years are more specifically professional training, including practical teaching experience. The fees at the teacher training colleges are lower than the secondary schools, a uniform 200 shillings per year, and many of the students at these institutions are there because they are unable to pay the larger fees at secondary schools. In general, however, the candidates for the teacher training colleges have received lower marks in the Primary Leaving Examination than their counterparts in secondary schools. There are close to 4,000 students enrolled in the teacher training colleges.

The third type of school is the technical school. There are five such schools enrolling a total of 1,000 students. The course leads to craft level in such skills as machine shop engineering, plumbing and building crafts. Fees in these schools are between 400 and 450 shillings per year. There are also a few rural trade schools, but these account for a very small part of post-primary training.

The final type of institution is the farm school, of which there are three, enrolling a total of 509 students. This is perhaps one of the weakest parts of a total educational system in a country that is almost exclusively agricultural.

Higher education after School Certificate (4 years of secondary school) is available in the Grade III teacher training colleges, the Uganda Technical College, and the Commercial College for those students who do not find places in the final two-year programme of the secondary schools.

The educational system is capped at the top with Makerere

University College, at the time of writing part of the University of East Africa. University education is paid for entirely by the Government of Uganda. The number of places available is quite limited. A number of Ugandan students find places in other African countries, the United Kingdom and the United States at the university level. Again, the importance of English should be readily apparent. But it should be noted that university education has more recently been diversified by sending students to socialist countries such as the USSR, Yugoslavia and China.

The material in the section Language in Education is an attempt to describe the language teaching policy in the schools, both in historical perspective and in terms of actual practice. It is also a description of the level of reading ability of pupils in Primary VII related to a number of sociolinguistic variables which are considered relevant to pupils' performance.

The data was collected in a variety of ways designed, at least in part, to furnish a means of checking the accuracy of the information obtained. The techniques included formal and informal interviews with education officers, headmasters, training college tutors and teachers; formal questionnaires; classroom observations and reading tests. The basic data on the schools was collected by 12 students from Makerere at 58 schools in 20 separate areas of Uganda. The interviews were conducted largely by the three members of the study team. A more complete discussion of specific instruments used to measure both reading ability and specific background information will appear in the following sections.

THE DEVELOPMENT OF LANGUAGE POLICY IN EDUCATION

The present language policy in the schools of Uganda as defined by the Ministry of Education in 1965 is not a new policy, but rather a definitive statement of existing practices which are largely a heritage of early missionary activities. Almost from the beginning of missionary activity in Uganda in 1877, the work of the missions was at least in part educational. Most Protestant missions required basic literacy as a condition for baptism and although the Catholics did not have the same requirement for baptism, they too included some literacy training in their missions, probably as a means of keeping pace with the Protestants. The missionaries

87

G

were instrumental in developing a written form of many of the indigenous languages in order to translate the Bible. One of the early missionaries, Alexander MacKay, began his work of teaching the fundamentals of reading and writing to the Africans while he prepared and printed a translation of St. Matthew's Gospel into Luganda.

From the earliest years of European contact with Uganda until 1924, education was solely in the hands of the missions, with each mission responsible for its own group of schools and teachers. Language policy was closely tied to one of the fundamental aims of Protestant mission educational policy which was to establish literacy in the language in which the Bible and prayer books were translated. The language of the schools was the language of worship. Early translations of the Bible were done in Luganda (used in Buganda and the Eastern Region), Lugbara, Ateso, Lwo and Runyoro/Rutooro. It was the preferred policy to use the local vernacular language, but in mixed vernacular areas like Bukedi, Luganda was used. Only in the very early years of missionary activity was Swahili used by the Protestant missions. (A translation of the Bible into Swahili had been done in Tanganyika.)

The colonial government did not begin to take direct responsibility for education until the mid-1920s by which time many mission schools were well established. When the government did begin to concern itself with education, its function was largely limited to providing financial assistance or establishing a few schools and training colleges.

British colonial policy regarding language was generally to provide primary education in the local vernacular language and post-primary education in English, with English taught as a subject in the primary schools. In 1928, Governor Gowers of Uganda, discussing the multilingual nature of the country, recommended the adoption of Swahili as the educational and administrative language of the Uganda Protectorate instead of Luganda, but the unpopular nature of the decision can be seen in the reaction of the Joint Parliamentary Commission on Closer Union which met in May 1931. The commission recorded that 'it would be desirable to encourage a gradual change from Swahili to English' after hearing African witnesses (all of whom were Luganda speakers) who were unanimously in support of English rather than Swahili.

The dislike of Swahili arose in part from the fears of Ugandans of the implementation of 'closer union' between Kenya and Uganda.

The Phelps-Stokes Report in 1924 was the first overall survey of education made in Uganda, and was perhaps the document most responsible for bringing education to the attention of the colonial government. The report was basically a description of the existing conditions in education at that time and made no mention of the language policy in the schools. The major recommendations of the report centred around the curriculum, urging greater emphasis on the practical needs of the country, including the teaching of agriculture in schools. Although the report itself was not concerned with language policy, there is little doubt that shortly after its publication the colonial government began to take a more active interest in education and as a result, the existing language situation was a subject of a memorandum in 1927. In general, language policy during this period was ill defined, but this first memorandum recommended very strongly that the vernacular should be the medium of instruction for primary schools with English introduced as a subject after the third year, or more specifically after children had attained a 'fair degree of facility in reading and writing in their own vernacular'. In general this meant that the first three or four years of primary school were conducted in the vernacular language with no English taught at all during that time. It should be noted that the memorandum did not mention any languages specifically although it defined vernacular as 'the language in which a pupil has learned from infancy to name the things he sees, hears, and handles'. The only exception to this policy which the memorandum recognized was in the case where small groups were surrounded by 'dominant vernaculars', but this again is not defined.

A report of the Commission on Higher Education in East Africa in 1937 made the following recommendations regarding language teaching:

(a) the teaching of English at all stages should be the subject of a special inquiry both locally and by the colonial government;
(b) the production of suitable textbooks in both English and the vernacular should be taken in hand.

The war years between 1938 and 1944 show no new developments in language policy. In fact, even the education reports are greatly abridged 'in the interest of wartime economy'. A series of general recommendations formulated in the early 1940s could not be implemented until after World War II due to lack of both funds and personnel.

The outline Scheme of Development for African Education, 1944–1954, touched only briefly on language policy. It states '. . . rapidly increasing numbers will enjoy a vernacular education . . .' and offers as one of its goals in the 10-year period '. . . to raise enrolment from 90,000 to 247,000 and to increase the numbers learning English from approximately 12,000 to nearly 70,000'.

In 1944, the Makerere Conference on Language was convened by the Director of Education to consider which of the many African languages should be used as languages of instruction in the schools. The conference decided on Luganda, Acholi, Runyoro, Ateso and Lugbara. It also accepted the view that English alone deserved recognition as the inevitable lingua franca of the future. It recommended the use of English as the medium of instruction from the seventh year onwards with its introduction as a subject in the third or fourth year of primary school. (The committee was divided in its opinion of when to begin teaching English due to the recognition of the inadequacies of existing conditions.)

In 1947, following the publication of the Colonial Office Memorandum (African 1170) on Language in African School Education, the Directors of Education in the four East African territories made the following recommendations regarding language policy:

(1) That the main vernacular in each area should be the sole medium of instruction throughout the primary range (I-IV) if it was sufficiently developed and widespread to justify the provision of the necessary textbooks.
(2) That local vernaculars, spoken in smaller areas only, should be used as the medium of instruction in the first class in their areas, after which children should be taught in one of the main vernaculars.
(3) That, since for most children not more than four years' schooling was available, there was considerable doubt about the advisability of introducing English as a subject below grade V.
(4) That it was desirable to intensify the teaching of English in the seventh year so as to make its use as an effective medium of instruction possible from the end of that class onwards.

In 1948, the Advisory Council for African Education reversed the decision of 1947 whereby English might be taught as a subject in class V or VI only, and said that they agreed that English should not be used as a medium of instruction in the primary schools except in exceptional cases, but felt that *no* restriction should be imposed

90

on the teaching of English before class V, provided that it had no detrimental effect on general education. The change recommended in this council was immediately put into effect by the Education Department.

For the first time, the language policy of the schools is clearly stated in the 1948 Education Report:

The language policy of the Department with regard to the use of the major vernaculars has remained the same, namely that six African languages are accepted as educational media in the primary school. These are Luganda, Lunyoro [sic], Lwoo [sic], Ateso, Lugbara, Swahili. From the point of view of the production of literature, it is clear that no further vernaculars can justify a claim to be regarded as a media throughout the primary school system, but the use of Lunyankole [sic] dialect of Lunyoro [sic] has been conceded in the first two years of the primary school in Ankole. This concession to the mother tongue has been made to the Kumam dialect in that area of Teso district and to Karamojong in the Kraal schools of Karamoja. The use of any language other than those included in the six listed above has not, however, been conceded in anything but the first two years of the child's school life.

This policy continued until 1952. A trend was beginning to develop for the earlier introduction of English and it was noted in the 1948 report that in private schools the teaching of English in the lower classes was often the greatest attraction in these schools, although the comment on this practice was that 'the advantages were not apparent'.

Nevertheless, by 1952 there was a decided change in opinion. The 1952 report says:

There is a very widespread desire for English to be taught at an earlier stage and for it to be used as a medium of instruction, even in the senior classes of the primary schools. The main obstacle to progress on these lines is the shortage of men and women who can teach English, but if this could be overcome, it would seem that the policy of introducing English as a school subject at an early age has much to recommend it. In the first place there are now a great many simplified readers for beginners; secondly, those responsible for teaching in the schools at post primary levels all say that the standard of English is too low for satisfactory progress to be made in the English medium in academic or professional subjects.

Another important language policy decision of 1952 was the announcement that Swahili was no longer a recognized vernacular in Uganda schools, with the exception of the schools for police and their children. The other five vernaculars accepted in 1952 were the same as those mentioned in the 1948 report.

The deBunsen Report of 1952 shows a continued interest in the wider use of English in the primary schools. It recommended that English be taught as a subject from class II as staff and material became available. The report also mentioned the need to train teachers to teach English and for a detailed study of the content and methods of English teaching in schools and training colleges. The committee also recommended the continued use of the five vernaculars which had been accepted by the Education Report of 1952.

The recommendations of the deBunsen committee are reflected in the Education Report for 1953. The report says that schools which have adequate teachers available are encouraged to introduce English as a subject at least as low as the fourth year.

There is also an awareness, seemingly for the first time, of the possibility of English medium instruction from the first year in areas which present special problems caused by the multiplicity of languages. There is a statement which reflects the thinking of the UNESCO Report on the Use of Vernacular Languages (1953) regarding the best language for education. The UNESCO report states that, 'We take it as axiomatic that each child should begin his education in his mother tongue'. The 1953 Education Report states:

Educational theory still maintains that it is necessary for the child to be taught in the early stages in its mother tongue. The difficulty in most parts of Uganda is that the multiplicity of vernaculars very often means that though a child does start instruction in a vernacular, that vernacular may not necessarily be its mother tongue.

In view of this, the report recognizes the need for experimentation in the field of English medium instruction, and offers examples of one school where non-English speaking children of workmen were given six months of special instruction in English and were then placed in regular classes at the Jinja European Primary School. The children were found to be able to proceed to the regular class with no difficulty.

During the next few years, the development of African education was based on the recommendations of the deBunsen Committee Report. Language policy remained essentially the same, with the implementation of the policy largely dependent on the availability of trained teachers.

In 1956, the first primary school built for children of all races was opened at Entebbe. The purpose of the school was to provide places for the children of African ministers who came to Entebbe from all parts of Uganda. Since the vernacular language used in the schools of Entebbe was very often different from the mother tongue of these children, an English medium school was established with the provision that children be fluent in English before admission to the school. Parents were responsible for providing private tutoring in English for their children to prepare them for entry.

In 1957 a special centre at Nakawa was started to experiment with the use of English as a medium of instruction for the lower classes of schools in Kampala. The aims of the project were:

(a) to provide a planned and balanced curriculum;

(b) to use the normal curriculum and activities of these classes as a basis for teaching English;

(c) to provide teachers with instruction in languages and teaching methods.

The project was undertaken with help from the Special Centre in Nairobi. The 1960 Education Report calls the experiment 'a marked success'.

The work of the Special Centre, Nairobi, should perhaps be explained in greater detail, since there is no doubt that it exerted great influence on policy and practice in Uganda. The Centre was set up in 1957 to prepare materials and teachers for an experiment with the use of English as the medium of instruction in the first year of primary school. In addition to the development of new materials, the programme brought with it a child and activity centred concept of education. The programme was first put into practice in a few urban schools for Asians and was an immediate success. An adaptation of the first set of materials for Africans was begun in 1961. Part of the success of the programme can be attributed to the fact that it solved many of the practical and political problems of educating children who came from widely divergent linguistic backgrounds. The appeal of such a solution to a country like Uganda is readily apparent.

At about the same time as the work of the Special Centre was going on, the Nuffield Research Project in the Teaching of English was in progress. This work was concerned largely with the problem of changeover from vernacular to English medium instruction in the primary schools. The rationale behind the work is summed up in the

93

following extract from the report by Peter Wingard:

It is useless to hope that merely by giving a daily English lesson for a given number of years, we can prepare children adequately for the use of English as the medium, and switch over completely when we think they know enough English. In most parts of Uganda, children have little immediate use out of school for the English they learn in school. One or even two daily lessons of English do not in themselves produce a high degree of skill and command of the language. The only way to acquire such skill is by actually beginning to use the English language for some real purpose.

The conclusions of the project were that there should be a gradual introduction of English as a medium and that the subject in which the changeover might best be made is probably Physical Education, where the teacher does most of the talking, the structures are commands accompanied by demonstration, and the vocabulary is the parts of the body, numbers, right, left, etc. Arithmetic, the subject most often used to make the switch over from vernacular to English, was felt to be unsuitable unless there was considerable attention to re-teaching the number bonds which had been learned in the vernacular.

The Commonwealth Conference on the Teaching of English as a Second Language held at Makerere in 1961 added its recommendations to the evolving policy of teaching English as early as possible. The recommendations of the conference were intended as guidelines for all of the Commonwealth countries, not only Uganda. The report notes the many problems involved in implementing an English language teaching policy, but acknowledges the growing trend that where a decision has been reached to use English as the medium of instruction 'the earlier (the language is introduced) the better'.

It then lists the following topics for investigation:

The psychological effects of a second language medium, including motivation; research into the needs and demands of the learner and community from the point of view of practical bilingualism; the influence of career prospects and personal and cultural example; the advantages and disadvantages of simultaneous and sequential bilingualism in the educational process; the age of introduction of English as a subject and the subjects to be taught through the vernacular; the influence of the English medium on the failure rate of students in other subjects than English.

One may well question on what basis the conference made its recommendations; and considering the magnitude of the problems, whether it had any clear justification for them.

The influence of this document as well as the pressure for the increased use of English is seen in the Castle Report of 1963, where the recommendations of the Castle Committee bring us to the present stage of the language policy in Uganda. Taken in historical perspective, there is nothing surprising in the report. The committee expands the number of vernaculars to six adding Runyankore/ Rukiga to the previous five: Akarimojong*/Ateso, Luganda, Lugbara, Lwo, and Runyoro/Rutooro. (It is not altogether clear what the committee meant by taking a pair of languages such as Akarimojong and Ateso and regarding them as one vernacular. As was shown in Part 2 of this book these pairs of languages are very closely related but are not identical.) The report goes on to state that children should normally be taught in their own vernacular in the early years of schooling except where circumstances make it impossible: e.g. where classes contain children of different race, tribe and language and in situations where lack of reading material in the local language makes the achievement of literacy in that language too difficult. It recommends the use of English as a medium of instruction in Primary V (the fifth year of school) and eventually in Primary IV. English should be introduced as a subject in Primary I.

The premise underlying the committee's recommendations is that if English is to be the language of instruction in post-primary education, then 'we accept the view of one of our witnesses that languages are best learnt through use, that is, through use as a medium'.

However, the evidence presented to the committee was by no means in agreement on some of these issues. The suggestion of Roland Hindmarsh on this point was that 'English as a medium should be Primary I or Primary VII. This means that the first six years of education shall be given through the medium of one language only—either English or vernacular'. Peter Wingard recommended the use of vernacular in Primary I to teach reading and writing while beginning oral English and using English as a medium for Physical Education and Arithmetic from the beginning. The Castle Committee does state that its suggestions are 'somewhat in the nature of a compromise between conflicting views'.

*An alternative form of Ngakarimojong. The author of this chapter is using the officially accepted form rather than that used by the people themselves, which was considered the more appropriate in Parts 1 and 2.

95

Despite this cautionary note, the major recommendations of the committee were adopted by the Ministry of Education and incorporated into the primary syllabus of 1965. English is introduced as a subject in Primary I and continues as a subject for all seven years of primary school. In Primary VI Mathematics and Physical Education are taught through the medium of English. English medium instruction is gradually extended to Science, Geography, Art, Crafts and Music in the fifth year, and in the sixth and seventh year all subjects are taught in English.

The teaching of English in the secondary schools is not rigidly defined by the Ministry of Education although there is a Ministry publication which appeared in May 1967 whose aim is 'to help schools achieve an effective and coherent course despite the inevitable frequent changes of staff'. Each school is responsible for the development of its own syllabus and scheme of work. The variability of the programme from school to school is restricted however both by the availability of recommended texts and the examination set for the end of secondary school. (English is a compulsory examination subject.)

English in the secondary schools is both a foreign language and a subject to be studied as a native speaker of the language would study it. Therefore, the English class includes work not generally necessary for a native speaker, such as oral language drill, and is forced to eliminate or simplify many elements of the curriculum which a native speaker would cover, notably in the field of literature. A large proportion of time must be devoted to the study of reading since it is a skill which is central to success in most other school subjects. (Although many literary works are studied in abridged editions, the texts which are available in various subject matter areas are the same as those used by native speakers at the same scholastic level.)

The recommendation of the Ministry of Education is for 9 periods of English a week; 3 periods of Reading, 3 periods for Writing, 2 for Language (grammar, etc.) and 1 period for Speaking.

It is impossible to estimate with any degree of accuracy the actual amount of teaching of other languages in the secondary schools. Figures are available for the 71 government aided schools, but there are a further 300 schools which are not within the government system and for which no statistics exist. Students enrolled in private schools are, however, eligible to take the School Certificate examinations. It is therefore possible to examine the figures for the examinations to see the number of students who sit the examinations in the languages in which there is a paper set. Table 3.1 shows these figures for three years, 1965, 1967 and 1968. (The figures for 1966 are unavailable.)

TABLE 3.1: *Numbers of candidates for English and for languages other than English in the School Certificate examination. Since English is a compulsory subject, the number taking English is the same as the total sitting the exam.*

Year	English	Luganda	Swahili	French	Latin	Gujerati	Punjabi	Hindi	Urdu	Arabic
1965	4,162	1,117	201	188	82	714	7	4	56	—
1967	6,225	960	295	392	60	684	8	16	39	—
1968	8,311	1,288	419	167	124	695	44	12	16	2

It may be seen that the number taking Luganda has remained about the same, despite the fact that the total number taking the examination has more than doubled. There may be political reasons for this; but it may be due to the recent alteration in the Luganda syllabus. It used to be possible for a non-Muganda to learn enough about the language to be able to pass this examination; and many Northerners did so. But now part of the examination requires a good knowledge of Luganda idioms and proverbs which is difficult for a non-native speaker to acquire. Luganda is taught in more schools than any other language, but they are almost entirely in Luganda speaking areas. In addition, although the figures do not show any present competition from French, in the future Luganda studies may suffer because of the increasing prestige of learning French or other European languages.

The proportion taking Swahili has remained almost the same. At present only one government aided secondary school offers Swahili as a classroom subject and one other has Swahili 'on a club basis'. Runyankore/Rukiga is being taught in two schools although no syllabus has, as yet, been set, and there is no paper at School Certificate level. There are plans to include this at a future date.

The teaching of Latin is generally limited to the seminaries. French is gradually gaining ground as an optional school subject, although this is not evident from the table. Several secondary schools now include French in the curriculum. The four Asian languages—Gujerati, Punjabi, Hindi and Urdu—are offered largely at Asian private schools.

In the Grade II teacher training colleges all students study one Ugandan language as a subject. The choice of language is determined by the location of the college. Each college teaches the official language of the district in which it is located. Primary school teachers trained in the Grade III teacher training colleges do not study any Ugandan language.

At the university level, only French and German are taught; French for three years, German for one (with plans to extend this in the near future). Teachers for secondary schools who study at Makerere University College have a one-year course in Language Methods in the Faculty of Education. This includes both English language teaching methods and methods for teaching Swahili, Luganda, French and German. In addition to the courses in the Faculty of Education, there is a new subject of Linguistics and African Languages with a one-year course (soon to be extended). English is taught at Makerere in much the same way as at any British university.

The official statement on language policy is not an accurate description of the situation in actual practice. At the district level, although there is a definite attempt to implement official policy, there is at the same time an awareness of the difficulties, especially in those districts showing the greatest linguistic diversity. An examination of Table 3.2 should serve to illustrate the complexity of the problem.

Table 3.2 shows the education districts and the official vernacular language of each. In several of the districts, the official vernacular language does not coincide with the major vernacular language spoken in the area. In others, large groups speak languages other than the official one. And even the most homogeneous districts have to cope with small pockets of people who speak languages other than the major vernacular of the area. Taking the country as a whole, about 40 per cent of the population are not native speakers of any of the officially approved school vernaculars. A further consideration in this regard is that people often live outside of districts where their own vernacular language is spoken, which

98

TABLE 3.2: *The education districts and the official vernacular language of each, including the major and minor languages spoken in the district.*

School District	Official Vernacular	Major Vernacular	%	Minor Vernacular	%
East Mengo	Luganda	Luganda	59	Runyarwanda	20
West Mengo	Luganda	Luganda	49	Runyarwanda	16
Mubende	Luganda	Runyoro	55	Luganda	28
Bugisu (incl. Sebei)	Luganda	Lugisu*	82	Sebei*	10
Bukedi[a]	Luganda	Ateso	26	Lugwere	22
Busoga	Luganda	Lusoga	71	Ateso	5
Ankole[b]	Runyankore/Rukiga	Runyankore	78	Runyarwanda	9
Kigezi	Runyankore/Rukiga	Rukiga	78	Runyarwanda	21
Toro[c] (incl. Bwamba)	Runyoro/Rutooro	Rutooro	53	Rukonjo	30
Bunyoro	Runyoro/Rutooro	Runyoro	81	Lugbara	5
Teso	Ateso/Akarimojong	Ateso	78	Kumam	12
Karamoja	Ateso/Akarimojong	Akarimojong	76	Suk	13
West Nile[d]	Lugbara	Lugbara	53	Alur	24
Madi	Lugbara	Madi	89	Kakwa	5
Lango	Lwo	Lango	94	Kumam	2
Acholi	Lwo	Acholi	93	Lango	3

Other vernacular languages in various districts:
  a Dhopadhola 17%; Lunyole 13%
  b Rukiga 8%
  c Rwamba 9%
  d Jonam 6%; Madi 7%; Kakwa 6%

*Lugisu and Sebei are, respectively, the official forms of the languages referred to earlier as Lumasaba and Kupsabiny.

means that even though their own language is officially used in the schools in their home district, their children attend school in an area where one of the other official languages is used.

Thus all of these variations from official policy must be considered in both planning and implementing the present language policy.

Often the problems involved in considering the needs of many of these small groups and the difficulties of teaching a child from a minor group in a language that is totally unfamiliar to him, have contributed to demands of both teachers and parents that English become the language of instruction as early as possible, even in Primary I. (In other words, if the child has to learn a new language when he goes to school, it might just as well be English right from the beginning instead of having him first learn a new vernacular and then switching to English further on in his schooling.) We will have more to say about this in a later section.

THE TEACHING OF ENGLISH—POLICY AND PRACTICE*

One of the major aims of the present policy is that by the end of primary school, pupils should be able to read anything written in simple English and that this skill should be permanent. A second facet of the programme is the preparation of a selected number of pupils for entrance to secondary schools, teacher training colleges, agricultural colleges and technical school. In 1967, only 21.6 per cent of primary school leavers found places in any of these post-primary institutions. The figure rose to 25 per cent in 1968. (This figure is not 25 per cent of the total age group, but 25 per cent of those who finished Primary VII. In other words approximately 10 per cent of all children in the eligible age group actually continued their education beyond primary school.) It is evident from these figures that primary education is terminal for the vast majority of pupils. It should therefore be remembered that the primary schools, in addition to their responsibility for preparing students to enter English medium post-primary institutions and assuring competence in the use of English, must also provide a sound basic education for the pupils who do not continue in school.

The successful implementation of the policy outlined in the previous chapter is dependent on several interrelated factors. First, and perhaps the most critical, is the availability of teachers trained to carry out the Ministry policy. The second is the availability of books and materials designed specifically for use with pupils from a wide variety of linguistic, ethnic and sociological environments who are learning English as a second, and sometimes third, language. Third is widespread understanding and support for the established policy. All of these factors, however, must be considered within the framework of the linguistic diversity of the country already outlined in the introductory section and examined in more detail in the second part of the book. We saw that there are at least 30 distinct vernacular languages spoken in Uganda. The Castle Committee recommended the use of only six vernaculars in the primary schools on 'educational grounds'. Perhaps their decision might more aptly be described in terms of basic practical considerations (i.e. the availability of books and teachers).

*The material in this section was written in conjunction with William Harrison of the Buloba Language Unit.

Despite the enormous logistic problems involved in implementing the policy of the Ministry, there is little doubt at the present that the question is no longer *whether* English should be taught, but *when* and *how* to do it most effectively. This leads us to a consideration of the other factors involved in the implementation of a language policy. Before considering these, it is useful to establish a set of criteria which might represent a hypothetical ideal in a total programme of teaching a second language for the purpose of using that language as the medium of instruction for all subjects. (It should be stressed that what is being discussed is the teaching of a second language as a practical tool of communication in the educational system, as opposed to foreign language instruction as a social or cultural asset.) This means that by the end of primary school, students should be sufficiently well versed in English to enable them to go on to do exactly the same things as native English speakers normally do in secondary school.

Unfortunately there is insufficient objective evidence to permit presenting any one method of language instruction as *the* correct method for achieving these aims, but the following principles derived from a number of sources, characterize what the authors believe is a relevant approach at the primary school level.

1. The teaching of a second language begins with a more or less protracted period of listening and speaking (aural/oral activity) during which no reading or writing is done. In a primary school course, reading and writing are generally deferred up to a year.

2. The course is organized around a sequence of structural patterns, logically arranged both on the basis of a contrastive analysis of the two languages and the difficulties within the target language itself. The principal advantage of contrastive analysis is to isolate the differences between the two languages in order to anticipate the major areas of difficulty.

3. In the early stages care must be taken to insure mastery of all of the sounds of the new language, especially those which are not present in the student's first language. Sounds are presented in the context of the structural material. Difficult sounds are given special attention.

4. A carefully controlled vocabulary which will be maximally useful in a realistic linguistic situation is presented in context.

5. Emphasis is placed on the kinds of activities which require

101

active participation on the part of the learner. Drills and visual aids are devised with the whole class in mind.

6. A great variety of drill material is given, mostly of the type which does not require students to use the textbook; the aim is to have automatic use of the patterns during the early stages of learning.

7. In teaching a foreign language, it is important to present a proper model for the students to imitate. If the teacher is not a native speaker of the language, the students should have as many opportunities as possible to hear native speakers on records, tapes, radio and as visitors to class.

8. Grammatical structures are taught through use rather than by memorizing rules. In cases where a formal rule does apply, it is presented in brief form and in non-technical language after the students have become acquainted with the structure through practice.

9. As much as possible drills are based on real situations with which the students can identify. The use of language which has no meaning to the students is avoided.

10. The texts are correlated with the aural/oral parts of the course. Here again, the subject matter should be relevant to the students and should take into account their maturity and experiences, as well as the purpose for teaching the language. The content should be related to the subjects the students will ultimately be expected to deal with when the second language becomes the medium of instruction.

The purpose of the list is not prescriptive, but is intended to furnish a useful basis on which to examine current practices in the primary schools in Uganda. Essentially, the foregoing principles cover three broad categories which overlap considerably. One has to do with teacher preparation and competence, the second is the actual material, including books, charts, practice exercises, audio-visual aids, etc., and the last is a combination of both teaching method and the underlying philosophy of education which it represents. Thus it may be said that any given set of material can be used in quite different ways according to the level of competence of the teacher and the attitude of the teacher toward the learning process, whether in fact she puts stress on the written aspects of language or the oral communication skills. Likewise, the essential aspects of a language programme may be appreciably altered by simply putting different sets of material into the hands of teachers who hold substantially similar views on education and who have comparable training and skill.

Each of these three categories—teacher preparation and competence, materials, and methods—will be examined separately, but the reader is again cautioned that it is almost impossible to regard any of these in isolation.

At present in Uganda, the primary schools are staffed by teachers whose training covers a wide range, both in the number of years of school attendance and the type of institutions attended.

Roughly 42 per cent of the teaching force are either untrained or hold a Grade I teaching certificate. This group includes teachers who have finished primary school (anywhere from 6 to 9 years) and may either have had no teacher training or attended a Grade I teacher training college. (There has been no recruitment of this kind of teacher since 1948.) The level of English of the Grade I and untrained teachers ranges from almost none to just adequate. Many of them have taken in-service courses to improve their own status. But for the most part, they are definitely not qualified to teach English.

Another 48 per cent of the teachers hold a Grade II certificate. These teachers have had between 6 and 9 years of primary school with 4 and 2 years of teacher training college, respectively. The most recent group have had 6 years of primary school, 2 or 3 years of junior secondary school and 4 years of teacher training in one of 26 Grade II training colleges.

The remaining 10 per cent are a mixture. Some are Grade III teachers who have had 2 years of teacher training after 4 years of secondary school. A few Grade III teachers were upgraded from Grade II after a 1- or 2-year course. There are a small number of Grade IV teachers who have been upgraded from Grade III after a one-year course in Great Britain or at Makerere. Then there are a number of individuals who are designated as graduates who have finished a university course but without special training in the teaching profession.

All of these differences, plus the presence of a small number of expatriate teachers, is an indication of the wide range of both training and competence that must be considered in planning the English language programme.

The important relationship between teachers and materials is

103

summed up very well by Brownell in his study of language teaching in Japan. He says:

Wherever highly competent teachers have the power to define the curriculum and select the materials, the instructional materials seldom become the determiners of all that is taught. But wherever teachers of modest or minimal standards of competence abound, there official syllabuses, textbooks, and other materials define the curriculum and control the teaching.

He goes on to say that in such circumstances teachers function as technicians who transmit the content of programmes designed entirely by others. And in a system where teachers are technicians, the role of the training college is more closely akin to a technical school, content to show how, rather than explain why.

Although Brownell's remarks relate to quite a different setting, his description is quite fitting in Uganda. The series of books adopted for use in the primary schools is essentially the core of the work covered by the teacher training colleges. Methods and materials become, in effect, one and the same. And for those teachers who are not graduates of training colleges, in-service work in English language teaching is also geared to how to use the current textbooks.

In a survey of 320 primary school teachers in 59 schools, 185 reported having had a special course in teaching English (in-service) or have had this as a part of training at the teacher training college. Many of the in-service courses were one-day workshops, although others extended for several weeks. One hundred and thirty-five teachers reported no special training, including some recent graduates of Grade II teacher training colleges. Closer questioning of some of these recent graduates, as well as interviews with the senior English tutors at many of the training colleges, indicates that the major part of the course designated as English Language Methods was in fact devoted almost exclusively to training the students to use the series of textbooks for the primary schools. Peter Wingard noted the same thing in a special report in 1962. He said then that 'almost all colleges (teacher training colleges) base their English method work solely on the textbook from which the teacher will teach'. Teachers who are trained in this method of teaching—teaching by textbook—are likely to use this same method once they are in front of their own class.

The practical implication of this kind of situation involves the potential for changing or improving the present language teaching methods. If teachers-in-training acquire the skills which they use in their own classrooms by emulating the methods by which they have been taught, then it becomes critical that the training college tutors be trained to use the best methods themselves. It would seem obvious that changing the type of teacher in the training colleges would begin to produce similar changes in the primary school classrooms.

In the present situation, the textbook becomes a mandatory course to be followed to the letter. There is uncritical acceptance of all of the material. In order for teachers to begin to use any set of material selectively and adapt it to local conditions they must learn that the written word is not infallible and that revision is both desirable and necessary. The most obvious disadvantage to the type of teacher training and preparation that rests so heavily on the course material to be taught is the fact that it encourages dependence on a single type of material and makes no allowance for the eventual (and probable) change to another series of texts.

Admittedly, there is some justification for this approach. For one thing it insures a certain degree of uniformity throughout the country. For another it affords a measure of security for the teacher whose level of competence in the use of English is not high. But the long-range effects of such an approach need to be carefully appraised. Each change in books will involve large scale in-service courses to prepare teachers to use the new text (a phenomenon already observed when the present series was introduced and later revised), and the total reliance on a single set of material, too often regarded by the teachers as gospel, tends to produce sterile, un-creative teaching and passive uncreative pupils. It also raises a rather serious question. What will happen to the money already spent on teacher training for the present series if (or when) a new series is adopted for primary schools?

Perhaps one of the most serious problems in the present situation is the teachers' own level of attainment in English. While no attempt was made to formalize a scale of attainment for rating teachers, a series of interviews and questionnaires indicated that the teachers themselves rate their own use of English as only fair, and an examina-tion of written responses to a series of questions reveals gross errors in both structures and spelling in English. Observations in dozens of classrooms indicate that even where the teacher has achieved good structural command of the language, pronunciation and intonation was never the same as that of a native speaker of English. Therefore, one of the most essential aspects of language teaching, a good model, is almost always absent. Nor is this compensated for by the use of tapes or recordings of native speakers. (Most of the secondary school pupils we interviewed said that they had never heard a native speaker of English until they reached secondary school and indicated that this was one of the most serious obstacles they had to overcome. This was also mentioned by secondary school tutors as one of their worst problems in working with new students.) The obvious result of the lack of a perfect model is that the pupils learn an imperfect sort of English from the beginning, and errors once learned are difficult to erase.

Then there is the problem of who teaches the English lesson in the vernacular teacher's class. In almost every case, the headmaster reported that Grade II teachers in the school were responsible for teaching English lessons for the vernacular teachers while that teacher took the other class for some other lesson, normally, but not always, the vernacular language lesson. In a few cases the headmaster said that he taught English in all classes where the teacher was unable to conduct the lesson himself. In a few cases, vernacular teachers themselves teach the English lesson, but this is only true when this teacher has taken special training in teaching English and applies in only a small number of cases, according to our sample. While this exchanging of classes is recognized as only a temporary, stop-gap measure to alleviate the shortage of fully trained teachers, it has numerous drawbacks. The English teacher comes into the class for a short time each day and there is no opportunity for the reinforcement of the English lesson in appropriate situations during the course of the day. If this teacher is absent from school it affects two classes instead of one. And the teacher himself has the added burden of getting to know two groups of children and preparing two sets of English lessons, one for a class he never knows as well as his own.

The teaching of the other school subjects in English is another formidable problem for the primary school teachers. It is a widely held belief (never subjected to careful experimental testing) that English is best learned by using it as a medium of instruction in other subjects. But here one must question whether a teacher with a limited command of English can possibly cope with the wide range of subject matter he is expected to teach in English. Aside

106

from the difficulties of specialized structural and lexical items (e.g. the earth turns on its axis, friction, electricity), there is the problem of teaching concepts often totally removed from the child's own experience. The net result in practice is that many lessons are taught in English with a subsequent translation into vernacular, a time-consuming and often wasteful practice. It is not uncommon to find children memorizing lists of items incorrectly copied into notebooks without any understanding of what has been learned. (A fact previously noted by Peter Wingard in the report of the Nuffield Research Project and by Edgar Castle in his book *Growing Up in East Africa*.) Clearly this kind of teaching is not producing the type of learning which is so necessary for subject matter mastery, nor can it be said to be serving the purpose of strengthening the use of English.

The problems of English medium instruction will be dealt with more fully later in this section. The point to be stressed here is that teachers are not sufficiently skilled in the use of English to insure the success of the programme.

With partially trained teachers, the choice of materials becomes central to the success of the present policy. The basic material for teaching English currently in use in Uganda is the New Oxford English Course, East Africa, adapted by F. G. French and R. J. Mason. This is a series of 6 paper-bound books with a teachers' manual for each book. The first few books in the East Africa series were published in 1958. The upper primary books appeared in 1960. Book One was revised by Gordon Watt-Wyness in 1964. The work formerly covered in Book One was expanded into two books to be used in Primary I and II. Book Two of the series was to be used in Primary III, etc., up to Book Six in Primary VII. Visual aids are intended to be used with Books One and Two, revised edition. These include pre-reading wall charts, reading cards, class pictures and sheets for individual apparatus.

In the main, the revised course for Primary I and II adheres to the basic principles of modern language teaching set forth above. Great attention is paid to speaking and understanding, with pupil activity central to the method used. The pupil's book for Primary I has multi-coloured pictures of objects and subjects familiar to the children. There is a minimal amount of written material, usually one word or a simple sentence under a picture. The book for the pupils in Primary II is also attractive and has more actual reading

107

material. There are numerous exercises in the book which require the children to identify a situation, read the sentence which describes it and indicate their understanding by writing the corresponding number in their exercise books. There are situations which are merely described by sentences below the pictures. Also included are songs, spelling, and a minimal amount of controlled composition. There are some paradigmatic situations with pictures in which the present progressive and past tenses are listed below. These pupil's books represent a considerable improvement, linguistically and pedagogically, over the original Book One.

In general, the hear-say technique is followed throughout Primary I. A very comprehensive set of language charts is used which incorporates high frequency vocabulary and structural items. All new vocabulary and structures are practised from the charts. Both individual and complete class responses are required. Because the materials are not based on contrastive analysis of any Ugandan language, they do not grade structure on the basis of the difficulties of the child's first language. There is, however, some attempt to grade structure according to their logic and difficulty within English itself. Thus 'yes/no' questions are taught before the 'what', 'where', 'why', and 'who' questions. The new material is activity oriented with games, and exercises included which have the ultimate objective or reinforcing phonological, structural and idiomatic items.

Much of the first year's work is pre-reading. The pre-reading materials are included despite the fact that the children are, at the same time, learning to read in their own vernacular language. There is some debate as to the validity of including this material, but the rationale of the author was that the children do not have pre-reading activities before learning to read in their mother tongues. It was felt that pre-reading activities in English would aid the children in all their reading activities.

While there is some adherence to structure control in the course, the language taught is introduced much too rapidly. In the first term of Primary I the children must learn the 'what' questions with objects and with 'do', and the indirect object (Give the book *to me*.), the 'who' questions, two nouns joined by 'and', possessives (This is the . . . of the . . .), the present tense with 'be', with action verbs, and with the present progressive tense. This grammar is taught along with a rather high number of nouns. This is typical of the course, and the result is a general lack of cohesiveness which steals some of its effectiveness.

The teacher's notes were also substantially revised and divided into two separate books, one for English language teaching and the other for English activity periods. One of the main flaws of the material is that it is quite difficult to coordinate the two books so that they complement each other. The teacher must decide for himself how to use the two parts and how to find activities that reinforce the material taught in the English language period. This is not only time-consuming for a busy teacher, but it also requires sophisticated linguistic and pedagogic knowledge on his part. Not a great many Uganda teachers in lower primary have the necessary training to perform these coordinating activities.

This problem is compounded by the fact that the two halves of the course are themselves not well coordinated. The language taught in one lesson isn't always reinforced by the activities intended to go with it. Thus, while the children are mastering basic question transformations in week four, the activity period presents sentences and questions using a different type of construction. It seems that a great deal of valuable learning time is wasted for this reason.

An additional characteristic of the teacher's notes is an unnecessarily complex method of giving directions to the teacher. This includes both the language used and the format chosen. A typical exercise may have a rather long, complex explanation to the teacher which is followed, in the exercise itself, by cues to the teacher (say, ask, repeat in chorus, etc.). If these simple cues were explained once in an introduction, they could then be used over and over within the body of material. As it is, the complex explanation often has the result of discouraging the teacher from using the notes at all. This is the most frequently stated reason for teachers using the pupil's edition for all classwork.

Despite these flaws, the newly revised course for Primary I and II represents a positive step toward a realistic, viable course for Uganda.

The format of the material in the subsequent books is essentially a short story, preceded in some books, by a section called 'Get Ready for Reading', and followed by a number of language exercises, e.g. questions about the story, word substitution drills, formation of plurals, spelling, etc., under the heading 'Seatwork'. The print is large and clear with eleven words to the line and 250 words per page. There is a small number of black and white illustrations.

Perhaps the first point that should be made about the New Oxford English Course generally, is that with the exception of Books One and Two, the series was not written specifically for Uganda. The present series is an adaptation of the Nigerian edition of the New Oxford English Course which appeared in 1957. The East African edition has been adapted in minor measure to the local situation by changing names of people and places and occasionally the content of a story, but the exercises are essentially the same in both sets of books. But again the series was not written on the basis of a contrastive analysis of even one of the local languages, let alone each of the six approved vernaculars. One series is expected to serve the linguistic demands of four separate language families— Bantu, Western and Eastern Nilotic and Sudanic!

Robert Jacobs makes a similar observation of the New Oxford English Course in use in Nigeria. He says:

The content and organization are based mostly on the authors' intuitive judgments and teaching or supervisory experiences in West Africa, and seem to overlook the linguistic data which are available, and which could be used more effectively in preparation of textual materials, e.g. anticipating particular difficulties which will be encountered in learning English by speakers of the various local languages.

Much of the vocabulary seems to bear little relationship to the vocabulary which is of use to students in real situations. It is neither practical from the standpoint of conversation, nor is it useful, in many cases, for providing a background for English medium instruction in other subjects. In addition, there is no way of knowing which words are new to the lesson either in the teacher's notes or the pupil's book.

The subject matter of the stories and the illustrative sentences seem far removed from children's practical needs for communication. Such practice sentences as 'Did he blow the engine whistle?' (Yes, he blew . . .) and 'What is the difference between a horse and a goat?' (a horse is totally unfamiliar to children in Uganda) are just two of many such examples.

Drill material is presented in such a manner as to require children to read lists of words down, up, and across. This is a very useless exercise at best, and one which certainly violates the principle of presenting vocabulary in context. Substitution drills require eye movements quite different from the normal left-right sequence needed for rapid reading and may be one of the contributing causes to the slow reading speeds of many of the children. An example of the first type of exercise taken from Book Four, page 2 is the following:

Instructions: Read down. Read up. Read across.

who	pick	find	cruel
whose	thick	found	camel
which	quick	ground	angel

Not only are the directions open to criticism, but one wonders on what basis the words are grouped together.

The second example comes from the same book, page 55.

	me		to buy
Please tell			to get
	that man	what	to throw away
He didn't tell			to take away
	us		to write

Ideally, drill material should be presented orally, which means that perhaps it should not even be included in the pupil's book. When one considers that frequently children see no other reader, it is indeed unfortunate that more space is not devoted to stories which the children can read. Most of the language exercises could be put on the blackboard by the teacher, thus saving space in the pupil's book which could then be devoted to much needed written material.

The exercises following the stories are often so repetitive that they encourage rote learning. In Book Four, 'The Story of Abdul' is followed by 5 exercises each of which require retelling the story, first orally and then in writing, proceeding from answering questions to filling the blanks to writing sentences in sequence to writing sentences about pictures—a total of 10 repetitions of the story plus the recommended reading and rereading.

One further example of the type of material and the way it is used should illustrate more fully some of the weaknesses already mentioned. The story in the pupil's Book Five (p. 102) is 8 pages long and consists of 11 numbered sections of one or more paragraphs. The subject of the story is a trip through big game country from Nairobi to Moshi along the Uhuru Highway. There are 5 black and white illustrations, four of which are photographs. The story is followed by questions on the reading. Each question tells the children in which paragraph the answer is to be found. Then there is an exercise on words ending -ght, another on the uses of the word 'too', and a third on sentence construction using adjectival clauses.

The teacher's notes for this story (p. 49 in the teacher's book) have a brief explanation of the Outward Bound Course which is mentioned in the story, a suggestion on the number of periods which should be allotted to each exercise, and brief notes on how to carry out each exercise. The general pattern of reading suggested in the introduction of the teacher's notes is for the teacher to read the story aloud explaining briefly in English or vernacular the words and idioms that are difficult for the pupils. This is followed by silent reading by the pupils and then oral reading by individual pupils while the whole class listens. The story is reread silently by the pupils following all of the exercises. The period of time suggested for all of this reading is 5 periods. (A period is 40 minutes.)

The 15 comprehension questions are allotted 2 periods. The teacher's notes have the answers for only 2 of these questions. The 18 words ending in -ght are to be used for dictation. The instructions read: 'Use these words for dictation. Put some of them into short sentences.' The section on the use of 'too' in the pupil's book says, 'The word too has two meanings:

(a) "more than enough"

I have too much food on my plate.

(b) "also"

I am going to the town. Will you come, too?

Write three sentences like (a) and three like (b).'

The teacher's notes say simply to make sure that the pupils understand the difference between 'too' and 'very' and give two illustrative sentences. One period is allowed for both the dictation and the sentences using 'too'.

The third exercise in the pupil's book requires using a section on page 194 which is a paradigm for sentences using relative clauses. The teacher is instructed to study the pattern with the class asking them to make up sentences orally using the pattern with words from lists appearing on pages 197 and 198. The teacher writes these sentences on the board underlining the 'adjectival' clause. The following period pupils write sentences of their own, either using the lists in the book or words of their own choosing. The pupils are told that their sentences must contain 'which', 'who', 'that' or 'whose'. The clause in English which employs these words is generally

112

referred to as a 'relative clause, although a relative clause is one of several 'adjectival' clauses.

The teacher's book has additional work not included in the pupil's book. There is a repetition of the previous dictation exercise, allowing another full period for this. It is followed by a section called 'Grammar, Oral' which allows 2 periods for the revision (review) of nouns, pronouns, verbs and adjectives, including both their meaning and their use. Two methods of revising are suggested. One is a team game with team A supplying a noun, team B a suitable adjective and team C making a full sentence. A second suggestion is to choose a paragraph from the story and have the pupils pick out all the nouns, pronouns, verbs and adjectives. During this activity, the teacher is also told to review subject, predicate and object. This entire section violates some of the most fundamental concepts of the modern approach to language teaching. Material is presented out of context. It bears no relationship to the way people speak, and it stresses the grammatical terminology rather than the function of words.

Following a final reading of the story, the teacher is told to set the pupils some 'true' and 'untrue' questions. In all, the children will have spent 13 lessons centred around a single story.

In actual practice there is often considerable divergence from the work that is outlined above. In one Primary VII class that was studying this story the teacher did not seem to be using the teacher's notes at all. The children took turns reading all of the questions on page 110 orally. The teacher then reread each question and had the pupils answer orally. The directions in the text at this level are for the pupils to *write* the answers to the questions. The work that was done in this class did not follow the directions, nor was it an improvement over the work as planned. In fact, the teacher seemed to be using a method suggested in earlier books which recommend oral work before written work. But this is clearly not intended at Primary VII.

In another class, the teacher used the dictation part of the lesson as an oral spelling lesson. He wrote the words on the board as the pupils spelt them aloud. There was some confusion over the spelling of 'height' and 'weight', probably because the list of words included such items as 'straight' and 'eight'. The teacher simply told the children to memorize the list.

The teacher's notes are a subject of great concern to almost

113

everyone connected in any way with primary teacher training or material production. The books are so poorly arranged that, in the words of one observer, 'they puzzle rather than help the teacher'. The most frequent criticism is that the teachers simply cannot read the instructions. The net result is that the teachers turn to the pupil's books and follow them the best they can, unable to supplement the material in any way.

The examples cited from Book Five are just a few of many where the instructions to the teacher are incomplete, often contradictory and extremely complicated. And in practice it results in the fact that the teacher simply lays the teacher's notes to the side and manages solely with the pupil's book. The notes are actually designed for a teacher who has a thorough knowledge of English and who can rely on his own knowledge to supply explanations and definitions when needed, as well as additional examples of specific grammatical structures. The teachers in Uganda are simply not fluent enough in their own English to be able to supply all of the material which is omitted in the notes.

The New Oxford English Course is used throughout Uganda except for occasional classrooms which use the New Peak Course (prepared for Kenya by the Special Centre in 1961). In almost all schools visited there were enough books available for every child. A very small number of schools reported that the books were in short supply, but this was always regarded as a temporary inconvenience rather than a normal condition.

Commercially produced visual aids such as charts, pictures, etc., are rarely available, especially in rural schools. The notable exception to this is in some of the demonstration schools attached to the teacher training colleges.

The situation in the larger urban centres is often significantly better regarding materials than in other areas. (One reason frequently given for this is the lack of locked storage space in many rural schools, which seems to preclude the acquisition and maintenance of any kind of supplementary teaching material.)

Another reason why many of the mechanical audio-visual aids are not found in the rural schools is the lack of electricity. While batteries are an acceptable substitute, in many cases the humidity results in rapid deterioration—hence a greatly inflated cost of operation. A further problem with mechanical equipment is the scarcity of trained maintenance personnel. Audio-visual aids, with

114

the exception of the transistor radio, are rarely available, and a radio was only available in about half of the schools we visited. (The presence of a radio is no guarantee that it will be used. Only a small number of the schools which we visited reported that they used the radio with any degree of regularity.)

The lack of audio equipment other than the radio means that the use of tapes or recordings of native speakers of English is not possible. The radio seems to offer a partial solution if it is used. The Ministry of Education broadcasts have a definite bias on language, both for lower and upper classes including a series of special broadcasts for Primary I, II and III teachers. The latter are designed to be heard the week before introducing the work to the class. (The necessity of adhering to a rigid timetable should be abundantly clear!)

A sample weekly schedule is included to show the type of programme offerings.

Tuesday, 2 July 1968
    11.00 a.m. English Lessons (Primary V and up)
    11.20 a.m. English Pronunciation 5 (Primary VI and up)
    11.40 a.m. English Lessons 5 (Primary V and up)
Wednesday, 3 July 1968
    11.00 a.m. English Stories 5 (Primary V and up)
    11.20 a.m. English Lessons (Primary IV and up)
              (Repeat)
    11.40 a.m. Science (Primary VI and up)
Thursday, 4 July 1968
    11.00 a.m. English Lessons (Primary V and up)
              (Repeat)
    11.20 a.m. School Certificate English 5 (Senior schools)
    11.40 a.m. Geography 5 (Primary VI and up)
Friday, 5 July 1968
    11.00 a.m. Science (Primary VI and up)
              (Repeat)
    11.20 a.m. French for Beginners 5 (Senior schools)
    11.40 a.m. Civics 5 (All grades)

But this is not the whole picture—the purist would perhaps argue (and in fact frequently has) that the broadcasts should be done by a native speaker of English, especially since this is often the only opportunity for all the pupils to hear native speakers. In actual fact, the purist seems to have lost the argument. The producers feel

that the element of dramatic competence is also of extreme importance, so that a person best suited for a particular role in broadcasting is in fact not always a native speaker, although level of
competence in the use of English is an important factor.

There was no opportunity to assess the impact of radio broadcasts
in English on the pupil's own use of English, but we suggest that
this is an area whose potential has not yet been fully exploited.

Perhaps one of the biggest single problems in terms of materials
is the lack of supplementary readers, a fact noted on several occasions
by training college tutors as well as from observations by other fieldworkers. *The New Oxford English Course* (henceforth NOEC)
by itself is incomplete. It is intended to be used with supplementary
readers, as noted both in the teacher's notes and the primary school
syllabus, but this material is simply not available in most schools. A
school with a library is a rarity. It is unrealistic to expect children to
develop good attitudes toward reading, not to mention the necessary
skills, unless they are given ample opportunity to read as wide a
variety of books as possible, both in and out of the classroom.

In the present situation in Uganda carefully developed material
assumes a position of extreme importance to compensate for
inadequately trained teachers. As Jacobs puts it, 'Materials must
serve part of the role normally served by teachers'.

The choice of method in teaching is determined to a certain
extent by the implicit beliefs in what constitute the goals of education. If one subscribes to the belief that there is a fixed body of
knowledge which is to be passed on from one generation to the next,
one can then accept the teacher as lecturer, the student as passive
listener. This has been the method largely used in the past and only
recently beginning to be challenged by new methods.

The gradual change in approach is not due to any single factor,
but rather to a combination of external forces, including the knowledge explosion which makes it virtually impossible to know all of
the information in even a single subject. Educational methods
reflect the change in emphasis from the passive learning of a body
of facts, to active participation in the process of learning—in
other words learning how to learn.

In language teaching this change in approach is apparent in the
present emphasis on using the language for communication rather
than learning the formal grammatical rules or concentrating on the
translation of long passages of prose. Ideally this means a relaxed

116

atmosphere in the classroom, encouraging actual speaking, an activity programme where children have the opportunity to use the language in real situations, greater emphasis on free use of language rather than slavish adherence to the book, and ample opportunity for practice.

Methods are, however, closely tied to both material and teacher training. Although a well trained teacher can usually compensate for poor material, it is doubtful whether good material can ever compensate for poor teachers. (The development of teaching machines and other audio-visual devices may cause us to change our thinking on this point.)

The methods used in teaching English in the primary schools shows wide variation, in some skill areas more than others. Some of the variation can be directly attributed to the level of training which the teacher has received as well as when the teacher attended school. But what appears to be even more significant than the level of training is the specific school where the teacher was trained and the method used by the English tutor who did the training. The influence of individual training college tutors on their students can be observed in many classrooms. On one occasion we had the opportunity of observing an English methods class at one of the training colleges. Shortly after this visit, we observed a school in the district and were struck by the similarity of the methods used by this classroom teacher and the training college tutor. After the lesson we spoke to the teacher and discovered that she was a recent graduate of the training college, and the tutor that we had observed had been the tutor of this particular teacher. This experience was in fact multiplied several times during the course of our travels around the country. Not all of the results are positive, however, since bad habits as well as good ones are just as likely to be copied. It is certainly a situation which deserves more carefully controlled observation, and one which has inherent the potential for introducing changes in the system.

Some of the teaching of language which we have observed makes use of what is more commonly referred to as 'the direct method'. That is, children are involved in learning the language by learning the connection between the word or words and the object or action which it represents. In other words, learning a new language through a process most nearly resembling the way in which children sponta-

117

neously learn a new language when they are exposed to a new language environment.

In an oral language lesson this might take the following form. The teacher has a number of common objects at his desk. He picks up an item and says its name. The children repeat the word. This is repeated several times, first teacher, then pupils in chorus, small groups and individually. This is both a way of teaching vocabulary and pronunciation. At a later stage the teacher uses a question and answer format—'What is this?' 'It is a ——.'

It has been our general observation that in Primary I and II, oral language lessons do adhere fairly well to this direct method. The problem in this case is not the method but rather the teacher's own language skill, e.g. pronunciation and intonation.

However, very often the methods observed in the classroom belong to no particular 'school of thought'. They have been an amalgam of methods either developed by the teacher on his own, taken from the teacher's notes or misappropriated from a variety of other sources, not the least of which is the teacher's own perception of how he was taught. All too often there is no method. A student reads, followed by another student reading, followed by oral and written questions. Very little attention is paid to oral language training, in many cases because the teacher doesn't know spoken English well enough or because a good oral language lesson requires a great deal of preparation.

It must be pointed out here that the methodology within the NOEC itself is eclectic—deriving from a number of sources rather than clearly following a single approach. The foundations of a strong audio-lingual course are set in the new material for Primary I and II. In the slightly revised material for Primary III and IV this is continued, though it gets diluted to a great extent here. In the upper primary course there is no method at all. The teacher's notes are a very slim supplement to the children's books which have reading passages followed by written questions and minimal language work. Thus, because the strong foundation is not followed up by equally sound materials, much of what is gained in the beginning is negated in subsequent years.

Another aspect of oral language—free communication—is more or less neglected at all levels, although both the syllabus and the teacher's notes encourage its development. From observations in many classrooms, an educated guess as to the reason for this

118

neglect is the teacher's lack of training in small group work. Ideally, conversation takes place among small groups of people and it is this type of activity which is most needed in the primary classroom, yet it is one area in which the present group of teachers is not prepared to operate.

The same small group situation described above is very effective for teaching reading, but again it is rarely observed. The teaching of reading is the area showing both the least diversity within the country and also the least creativity. The pattern is most often for the teacher to read an introductory paragraph, followed by silent reading by the whole class, followed by individual oral reading until the whole story has been read aloud by the whole class. In one story in Book Four of NOEC it is estimated that the children reread, retold and revised the same 2-page story 12 times before finishing the lesson. This may have advantages for the development of other language skill; however, it is a decided drawback in promoting interest and skills in reading!

The organization of the timetable for teaching English is another point which must be mentioned because it reflects the basic attitudes of the programme planners toward the teaching process as well as indicating the areas which are to be given the greatest emphasis.

Primary I: ten 20-minute periods per week
5 of English language—oral
5 of English activity—pre-reading, games, etc.

Primary II: ten 30-minute periods per week
5 of English language—reading and writing
5 of English activity—individual reading apparatus, games, etc.

Primary III: ten 30-minute periods per week

Primary IV: 7 of English language—NOEC
3 of English activity—oral composition, story telling, dramatization, supplementary reading

Primary V: eight 40-minute periods per week
5 of English language—NOEC
3 of English activity—oral composition, some written work and supplementary reading

Primary VI: six 40-minute periods per week

119

Primary VII: 3 of English language—NOEC (Book Five up to
Chap. 13,
Primary VI)
(Primary VII—
Book Five to
end)
3 of English activity—written work, poetry,
plays, supplementary
reading, special activities
(debating, newspapers)

It can be seen from the above schedule that the use of the NOEC forms at least half of the work at all grade levels. An average week's work in NOEC itself contains 2 or 3 lessons specifically geared to the teaching of reading skills—hardly enough time to develop adequate reading skills, a fact attested to by the secondary school teachers.

A report written by Watt-Wyness of the Inspectorate Division of the Ministry says: 'All Secondary Schools talk of this inability to read with understanding.' (If this is true of the highly selected group who enter the secondary schools, how much more does it apply to the primary school leavers.) 'We should insure that these children can go on reading in English for the rest of their lives, otherwise we are allowing a tragic waste of the nation's resources.'

An examination of the total ELT programme in Uganda reveals several gaps between the ideals of second-language teaching and the actual practice. Briefly, they may be summarized as follows:

The Teacher
    1. level of English not sufficiently high
    2. lack of specific training in TESL

The Material
    1. present course not adequate on several grounds
    2. teacher's notes difficult to understand
    3. material is unrealistic and often artificial
    4. lack of supplementary readers
    5. lack of audio-visual equipment

Methods
    1. heavy reliance on rote learning
    2. little opportunity for spontaneous speech
    3. too heavy emphasis on oral reading
    4. insufficient time to cover material

Some, if not all, of these weaknesses in the present programme were anticipated by programme planners, even before the present syllabus was put into use. Certainly the Castle Committee recognized that a massive programme of in-service training would be necessary to raise the level of performance of the teachers already in the classrooms before the recommendations of this committee could be put into operation. At the same time, efforts to raise the standard of training for new teachers were planned.

In-service education is the responsibility of the Central Inspectorate, which undertakes programmes both on its own and in conjunction with a number of other agencies. The courses offered by the Inspectorate in most cases relate to the needs of a national type—introducing a new syllabus, upgrading of teachers, etc. With the introduction of English as a medium into lower classes of primary, courses were offered throughout the country to help teachers understand the aims and objectives of the new approach. The same type of courses were organized when the revised Books One and Two of NOEC were introduced. Many of the courses of this type are one-day or weekend courses.

Several agencies work closely with the Ministry and Central Inspectorate to supplement the in-service training programme. The British Council organizes courses in the field of English language teaching and provides both personnel and funds for the support of such programmes. It also assists in the preparation of teaching material and supports library growth by providing books and technical assistance needed for setting up and maintaining library services.

The National Institute of Education is also involved in the in-service training field. The Institute functions in part as a coordinating body between Makerere University College and the Ministry of Education. Much of the work of the Institute is in up-grading of teachers who have already had some professional training and experience. But the Institute also provides in-service courses in various subject areas and is additionally concerned with demonstration teaching, workshops and material production. A further function of the Institute is in the field of research in education.

UNICEF is also involved in the field of in-service education. At present UNICEF is sponsoring an extensive up-grading course for vernacular and Grade I teachers. The major emphasis of the course is English and is a combination of vacation courses (residential) and correspondence instruction. At present 1,000 teachers are

121

enrolled in the second year of the first of such 3-year courses. All of the Grade I teachers will eventually be included in this programme.

Additional in-service work is conducted at Buloba College, the first of 4 regional in-service centres. There is a permanent staff at Buloba and teachers from all parts of the country come for courses lasting from 4 to 9 weeks. The major emphasis of the programme is overall teacher improvement, sometimes concerned with specific problem areas, such as infant methods, and English medium instruction for upper primary classes.

There are two training centres, one at Ggaba and one at Ngora, which are specifically for up-grading Grade II teachers. Experienced teachers who are selected by examination spend two years doing additional work in all subjects and then receive their Grade III certificate.

In addition to the in-service work being done, a number of external agencies supplement the work being done in teacher training. Teacher Education for East Africa (TEEA), a programme administered by Teachers College Columbia University and funded by the U.S. Agency for International Development (USAID), provides training college tutors directly to many teacher training institutions including the National Institute. In 1968 there were 34 tutors in 18 teacher training colleges. Of these, 14 tutors are designated as English or Education specialists although most of the tutors do teach some English courses regardless of their speciality. The tutors become employees of the Ministry of Education and are under the direct supervision of the principal of the college to which they are posted.

An additional number of teachers are posted to the teacher training colleges by such agencies as the British Ministry of Overseas Development, the Canadian Government and various Scandinavian Government volunteer schemes. Many of the staff of the teacher training colleges are posted by various missionary organizations. In 1966, 138 teachers in the teacher training colleges (50 per cent) were supplied by external agencies.

Plans are currently under way to construct four regional training colleges, meant to supplant the present Grade II training colleges. These colleges will recruit students who have finished 4 years of secondary school and will train Grade III teachers. The initial plans and projections were funded by USAID loans and grants.

It is apparent that there are a number of very serious problems in the present system which decrease the efficiency of the policy of teaching English and using it as the major means of instruction in the schools. Yet despite the difficulties, some children do learn to read, write, speak and understand English well enough to proceed into secondary schools and later universities. Some schools have a higher success rate than others within the same system.

The next section is an analysis of a number of sociolinguistic factors which appear to contribute to these differences in an effort to determine some of the relationships between these factors and one phase of English language competence—reading achievement.

THE TEACHING OF ENGLISH—REALITIES

The purpose of this section is to describe the reading achievement of a sample of Primary VII children in Uganda and to relate this achievement to a number of sociolinguistic variables.

The questions which this study attempts to answer are:

(1) Do children who live in urban areas do better than children in rural areas in Uganda?

(2) What are the differences in reading achievement based on the grade in which English language instruction was begun?

(3) What effect do age, sex, language background, aspirations, parents' language background and occupational level have on pupil achievement in reading English?

(4) What is the effect of teacher training and experience on achievement?

SELECTION OF THE SAMPLE

The schools in the sample were in areas of the country selected within the framework of the larger survey. (See Part 1.) A total of twenty rural areas were studied in eleven different administrative districts. Ten of the areas were linguistically homogeneous; ten were either heterogeneous or were composed of a minority linguistic group within a major linguistic group area. Within each of these areas two or three schools which scored in the middle range for the district on the 1967 Primary Leaving Examination were selected with the help of the District Education Officer. (The average score on the Primary Leaving Examination, English sub-test, was 61.00 in the country as a whole. The average score of the schools in our

123

sample on this same test was 60.63.) Nine schools from Kampala were also included in the sample. These schools were selected to represent the complete range of schools in an urban area.

The tests were administered to all children in the Primary VII (seventh grade) class in the schools. There were a total of 58 schools, 49 of which were rural. (The potential total of rural schools was 60—five from each of 12 fieldworkers—but due to illness and other unpardonable sins, some of the work was not completed.)

THE READING TEST

A reading comprehension test was developed to establish a relative measure of English language competence against which relationships with the other variables could be determined.

Part I—English

The test reflects a level of attainment considered desirable by the end of primary school, i.e. what the pupil could be expected to read when he finished Primary VII. It included a total of five passages, two from a Secondary 1 reading textbook with a 2,000 word controlled vocabulary, one from a Primary VII Civics book, one from the local press and one from a reading workbook at a slightly easier level than the other material. Each of the passages is followed by five multiple choice questions with four possible answers. (See Appendix.)

All of the items were pre-tested individually in a number of Primary VII classes and several Secondary 1 classes. The items were all answered correctly at the Secondary 1 level, and the test was considered, therefore, to be a reasonable measure of the level of reading desired at the end of primary school. (While all Secondary 1 pupils whom we tested scored perfectly, it should be remembered that these pupils represent the top 10 per cent of last year's Primary VII class.) Item one (see Appendix) was very easy for most of the Primary VII pupils, but it was included because it was felt to be a useful introduction to the test and one which would provide some measure of success for all pupils.

Part II—Vernacular

A passage in a vernacular language was also included in the

test for three reasons: (1) to see if there was a relationship between the ability to read English and the ability to read a vernacular language, (2) to assess how well children could read the official vernacular language of the district, both when this was and when it was not their own first language, and (3) to see whether, over the country as a whole, children could read better in English than in a vernacular language. The passage which appeared in translation was taken from the same Civics textbook referred to earlier.

Both passages from the Civics book were of comparable difficulty (pre-tested) in English. Both passages were translated from English into each of the six official vernacular languages used in the schools by a student at Makerere University College who spoke that language as his first language. The passages were then translated back into English by another native speaker of the language and corrections in the text were made as needed. As a final check, the item was given to another speaker of the language to make sure that all the questions were being answered correctly. This item was not field tested with Primary VII pupils before it was given.

One half of each class received the test with passage A (Agriculture) in English and passage B (Forests) in the official vernacular language of their district, the other half received item B in English and item A in the vernacular language. The tests were randomly distributed to the pupils in each class.

The test was designed with specific printed instructions for administration to be read aloud to the pupils and included a practice exercise in the method of marking the correct answers. All of the fieldworkers who administered the tests were given one practice experience in giving the test to a Primary VII class.

There were no other test scores for these children against which this reading test could be evaluated. Teacher estimates of individual levels of attainment for pupils proved unreliable in many instances because the teachers are not in the habit of evaluating a pupil's performance. In a few cases where teacher evaluation was attempted we got a very high degree of correlation between performance on the reading test and teacher's judgement of English language ability. In other cases there was no correlation at all. Frequently the names on the teacher's list did not even match the names of the students who had been tested.

125

THE LINGUISTIC QUESTIONNAIRE

A linguistic questionnaire was also developed to provide information on the individual pupils. (See Appendix.) The problem was finding a form that required little writing and simple directions. A problem which caused a substantial amount of trouble was the direction 'Put a tick (check) "in front of" ...' For reasons not entirely understood, this often was interpreted as 'after' or 'behind'. This frequently meant that the intended answer was not clear.

Most of the items in the questionnaire are self-explanatory; a few need some interpretation. All of the information represents selected sociolinguistic variables to be correlated with the results of the reading test. Item 1 which asks the child to list his schools, is designed to assess the child's mobility. A simple question about how many schools the child attended did not supply all the information we wanted. By using the list we gained such information as the number of years in each school, the mobility within a district and mobility between districts. Item 2 which asks for the child's first language and item 3 which asks which language the teacher used in Primary I supply information about whether the child's vernacular language coincided with the school vernacular. The question implicit here was whether the child who must learn a second vernacular language before learning English is handicapped in any way.

Item 9 was originally worded 'What will you do when you finish Primary School?' In the original group of 300 students on which this item was pre-tested, 100 per cent of the pupils checked 'Go on to Secondary School'. Teachers and headmasters felt that this was an accurate picture of the aspiration level of the children. It is possible to infer from this that aspirations are high among the children who have reached Primary VII. The question was reworded to see what alternatives the children would see to a full secondary education.

OTHER QUESTIONNAIRES

A questionnaire was distributed to each teacher in every school. A separate questionnaire was given to the headmaster. Frequently the headmaster has a full teaching position in addition to his administrative responsibilities, in which case he received both questionnaires. The purpose of these questionnaires was to elicit both general information about the school (e.g. the vernacular

126

language used in teaching, the foundation body, and whether a Grade III teacher was teaching the present Primary VII class), as well as specific information about the teaching background of the staff (e.g. the Grade Ministry Certificate held by the teacher, the years of teaching experience, and the years in the present school). Copies of these questionnaires are in the Appendix.

THE COLLECTION OF THE DATA

The tests and questionnaires were administered by 12 students from Makerere University College, five from the English Department and seven from Social Sciences. The students spoke the language of the area in which they did their field work; they also spoke English.

The students worked on the project during their long vacation from 25 March 1968 to 14 June 1968. During the first two weeks, the students were trained in field work methods by the three members of the Survey team. During this training period they were taught to administer the reading test and linguistic questionnaire. From the 8th to the 26th of April the students travelled to selected areas gathering data, and as one part of this field experience gave the reading test in one school. This was a trial run.

The students returned to the campus to review the results and prepare for the second phase of the field work. During this second field experience they gave the reading test in two separate areas; three schools in the first area and two schools in the second. During the final week of the vacation period, the work was reviewed and results were tabulated with each fieldworker and one member of the Survey team.

The reliability and validity of the field work is, of course, variable, since it depends on the individual student fieldworkers. But checks were made on the quality of the work that was being done. During each of the field work experiences, each student was visited at least once by one of the three members of the Survey team.

ANALYSIS OF DATA

The question which is implicit in a study of this kind is: what factors are relevant to the success of the present language policy in Uganda? A knowledge of the conditions which are most likely to produce successful candidates for entry to post-primary institutions

127

allows for programme improvement in the appropriate places. The value of knowing which environmental factors, alone or in combination, are most relevant to an individual's success permits the development of new programmes based on sound evidence. The relevance of such information in any system needs hardly be mentioned, but in a country that is still in the process of recreating both its educational system and teaching materials, this knowledge is even more important. The statistical data presented in this chapter indicate some of the major factors which must be considered in planning new material and carrying out experimental programmes.

Overall Performance

The reading test was administered to a total of 1,560 Primary VII pupils in 58 schools in Uganda. The mean score was 15.85 with a standard deviation of 3.55. Out of a possible score of 25, the range of scores was from 6 to 24. Children who scored very low on this test might have done so for a variety of reasons not related to their ability to read English, such as losing their pens or having malaria; and children who scored very high might equally not be representative of the group as a whole because of reasons such as having lived in England. In order to be more sure of our conclusions about Ugandan children as a whole, we followed a common statistical practice of discarding all scores which fell more than 2 standard deviations above and below the mean, i.e. scores above 22 and below 9. In all, 66 scores were not evaluated in the final sample. The corrected mean for the 1,494 remaining cases was 16.04 with a standard deviation of 3.08.

The following table shows the mean scores of the schools in the sample, including the district and major vernacular language spoken in the school, as well as the score on the Primary Leaving Examination English paper for 1967.

TABLE 3.3: *The district, major vernacular language, mean score on the English section of the reading test, and mean score on the Primary Leaving Examination English paper for 1967.*

	District	Language (School)	English Score	P.L.E. Score (Eng.)
1.	Teso	Ateso	15.48	59.22
2.	Teso	Ateso	16.56	63.23
3.	Teso	Ateso	17.43	57.71
4.	Bukedi	Ateso	16.90	62.08
5.	Bukedi	Ateso	19.41	61.21

TABLE 3.3:   (*continued*)

	District	Language (School)	English Score	P.L.E. Score (Eng.)
6.	Bukedi	Luganda/English	16.45	68.79
7.	Bukedi	Luganda	15.00	57.97
8.	Bukedi	English	16.75	62.79
9.	Bukedi	Dhopadhola	16.35	75.28
10.	Bukedi	Lunyole	15.83	62.92
11.	Bukedi	Luganda/Lunyole	16.00	62.66
12.	Karamoja	Akarimojong	17.33	55.77
13.	Karamoja	English	18.05	69.40
14.	Toro	Rutooro	15.96	58.72
15.	Toro	Rutooro	15.37	62.40
16.	Toro	Rutooro	15.42	61.78
17.	Toro	Rutooro	14.44	62.57
18.	Toro	Rutooro	16.37	—
19.	Mubende	Luganda	14.16	53.27
20.	Mubende	Luganda	13.65	47.14
21.	Mubende	Luganda	14.05	57.32
22.	Mubende	Luganda	12.28	53.46
23.	Mubende	Luganda	15.05	55.89
24.	Kigezi	Runyarwanda	17.20	54.29
25.	Kigezi	Runyarwanda	18.65	69.08
26.	Kigezi	Runyarwanda	17.10	67.03
27.	Kigezi	Rukiga	15.39	59.09
28.	Kigezi	Rukiga	16.45	63.70
29.	Kigezi	Rukiga	16.88	61.73
30.	Kigezi	Rukiga	14.66	61.73
31.	West Mengo	Luganda	13.96	55.94
32.	West Mengo	Luganda	15.82	57.04
33.	West Mengo	Luganda	13.35	54.59
34.	Lango	Lango	15.32	69.09
35.	Lango	Lango	13.68	60.56
36.	Lango	Kumam	16.44	63.29
37.	Lango	Lango	14.15	58.66
38.	West Nile	Alur	14.50	49.23
39.	West Nile	Alur	15.76	54.06
40.	West Nile	Lugbara	17.62	62.66
41.	West Nile	Lugbara	17.60	63.14
42.	West Nile	Lugbara	16.75	—
43.	Ankole	Runyankore	16.11	65.81
44.	Ankole	Runyankore	14.96	60.52
45.	Ankole	Runyankore	15.17	68.45
46.	Bugisu	Luganda/Lugisu	16.79	63.44
47.	Bugisu	Lugisu	17.07	62.32
48.	Madi	Kakwa/Lugbara/Madi	14.16	50.81
49.	Madi	Madi	14.42	58.00
50.	Kampala	English	14.92	55.60
51.	Kampala	English	15.20	60.50
52.	Kampala	English	16.39	63.26
53.	Kampala	English	17.36	67.09
54.	Kampala	English	17.55	68.49
55.	Kampala	English	18.37	77.70
56.	Kampala	Luganda	17.90	59.79
57.	Kampala	Luganda	16.36	59.95
58.	Kampala	English	14.68	58.00

Forty-nine of the schools are in rural areas; nine of the schools are in Kampala. The schools in Kampala are of three main types: two are predominantly Asian schools which use English as the medium of instruction from Primary I; two are African schools which use Luganda as the medium of instruction in the lower primary classes and teach English as a subject from Primary I; and five are predominantly African, but mixed linguistically, which use English as the medium of instruction from Primary I. The latter group includes schools which draw their pupils from different socio-economic groups—some being in housing estates (middle income) and others in migrant areas (poor).

Ten of the schools are English medium from Primary I, seven in Kampala and three in rural areas. (These schools have frequently started using English as the medium of instruction within the last two or three years, especially those schools in the rural areas.) Thirteen of the schools use a vernacular language that is different from the official language of the district as the major language of *oral* instruction in the lower primary classes. Reading is taught in the official vernacular language.

Table 3.2 (above) shows the scores on the reading test and on the English paper of the Primary Leaving Examination. It can be seen that scores on the reading test are related to the level of proficiency in English in the school as measured by the results in the Primary Leaving Examination for 1967, indicating that schools which do well in teaching English continue to do well in producing pupils who achieve well in English, and schools which do poorly continue to do poorly. Twenty-one of the schools have scores above the mean in both the reading test and the Primary Leaving Examination English Paper. Twenty-three of the schools have mean scores that are lower in both tests. In seven schools the Primary Leaving Examination score is higher than the mean, but the reading score is below, and in five schools this is reversed. Information on two schools is incomplete. The two sets of scores are highly related, a fact which is readily seen by comparing the two sets of figures and which is also verified by statistical analysis ($r=.68$; $p < .001$). There is a strong indication that schools which have been successful will continue to produce pupils who are better in English than the schools which have not been successful.

The distribution of school scores as a whole approached a normal distribution with some skewing to the left, probably because the test scores were constrained from above. There was no obvious bimodality of the scores. The means and the variances of students' scores within a district were correlated —.4, and this again is probably the result of the constraint from above on test scores.

The Relationship between Selected Sociolinguistic Factors and the Ability to Read English

In order to examine some of the sociolinguistic factors which affect a pupil's ability in English, the top scorers and the bottom scorers were selected for comparison, and X^2 analysis of the data was done. There were 203 pupils in each of the two groups; the top group had scores of 20, 21 and 22 on the reading test; the bottom group had scores of 9, 10, 11 and 12.

Language of Instruction in Primary I The first assumption, based on the growing tendency to begin English medium instruction as early as possible, was that most of the high scorers would come from schools where English had been used as the medium of instruction from the beginning of Primary I, indicating the superiority of this method over any other. The distribution of pupils is shown in Table 3.4. There is no difference between the two groups of pupils in terms of whether they learned in English from the beginning or whether they began with their vernacular language.

TABLE 3.4: *Distribution of high and low scorers on language of instruction in Primary I.*

	English	Vernacular
High scorers	24	179
Low scorers	21	182

When Child Learned English The second assumption, also based on the principle that the earlier children begin to study English the better they will do, was that children who began the study of English as a subject in Primary I would do much better than children who started later. Table 3.5 shows the distribution of high and low scorers according to when they began to learn English. While it is evident that a larger number of children who learned English at home are in the group of high scorers, this offers no useful information for the purpose of evaluation of instructional programmes. It may indicate that pre-school training in English is beneficial, but it says nothing about when to introduce English in school. There is some indication from these data that the earlier one begins the study of English the better one does. What is more important to note is that none of the high scorers began the study of English as late as Primary IV.

TABLE 3.5: *Distribution of high and low scorers according to when they began to learn English.*

	At Home	PI	PII	PIII	PIV
High scorers	17	64	41	75	—
Low scorers	6	53	47	85	11

The scores of the entire group (1,494 cases) on this same factor show a slightly different picture. Table 3.6 shows this distribution. The mean score of the group that learned English at home is still

TABLE 3.6: *Distribution of the entire group showing when they began to learn English.*

	No. of Cases	Mean Scores
At Home	80	16.96
Primary I	455	16.16
Primary II	300	15.82
Primary III	585	16.00
Primary IV	74	15.41

significantly higher than the mean of the group as a whole ($t=10.39$) and the mean of the group that learned English in Primary IV is significantly lower than the mean of the group as a whole ($t=6.69$). But the other three groups are *not* statistically different from each other.

Sex   An analysis of the data for the entire group as well as a chi-square analysis of the high and low scorers does not reveal any significant difference in performance between males and females.

Home Background   There were no significant statistical differences between the high and low scorers on whether the father or mother spoke English. This was further supported by the fact that there were no statistical differences between the high and low scorers based on father's occupation. However, an analysis of the data for the entire group indicates that children of professionals score significantly higher than the mean of the entire group ($t=8.84$). Children of professionals are more often in schools in Kampala, a factor which will be considered further on in this chapter.

Aspirations   As was mentioned earlier in the paper, the pupils who reach Primary VII all aspire to continue their schooling, from which we conclude that aspirations are high at every level of achievement. When pupils were given a second choice, and these choices were grouped into school and non-school categories, the

132

chi-square analysis showed no significant differences between the high and low groups.

Mobility The data for the entire group showed no significant difference in the mean scores for children who moved to different schools within the same district, but children who moved to different districts scored significantly higher (t=7.88). Table 3.7 shows the mean scores for the different groups based on mobility. The percentage of pupils whose fathers were professionals was 14.1 per cent in the group who moved to different districts as opposed to 12.8 per cent in the total sample.

TABLE 3.7: *Mean scores based on mobility of pupils.*

	Cases	Mean
Same school 7 years . . .	793	16.00
Two schools	331	16.04
More than 2 schools . . .	285	15.90
Different districts . . .	85	16.75

Age There are slight differences in performance based on the age of the pupils, but these differences show up in only the youngest and oldest pupils in the sample. The differences are not statistically significant between the high and low scorers. These figures are shown in Table 3.8.

TABLE 3.8: *Distribution of high and low scorers by age.*

	11	12	13	14	15	16	17+
High . .	11	22	35	46	20	11	2
Low . .	2	20	39	56	20	4	2

The analysis of the data on age for the entire group also shows the 11-year-olds to have an advantage, but not the 16-year-olds. The following table shows the mean scores for the whole group according to age. Only the scores for the 11-year-olds and those 17 or older are significantly higher than the mean score for the group as a whole. The number in both groups is too small to be of any real significance. Of the 31 eleven-year-olds in the sample, 18 were from Kampala and 13 were from rural schools.

Thirty per cent of the eleven-year-olds come from homes where the father is either a teacher or professional. One can speculate that all eleven-year-olds who are in Primary VII started school at a very early age because they were identified as being exceptionally bright.

TABLE 3.9: *Distribution of mean scores by age groups.*

No. of Cases	Age	Mean Score
31	11	17.80
160	12	16.05
330	13	15.91
344	14	15.95
126	15	16.22
52	16	16.07
13	17+	16.92
(438 cases—age unknown)		

For all of these reasons, it is impossible to generalize that all children should start primary school at the age of 4 or 5.

Nor is it possible to generalize about the group 17 or older. There are only 13 cases to consider. All of these are from rural areas where the fathers are either farmers or unskilled workers. There are two possible explanations for the fact that these students do so much better than average. The first is that many of them may be repeating Primary VII and therefore have had an additional year (or more in some cases) of English instruction. The other explanation is that having been more mature when they started primary school they learned more quickly than their younger classmates.

There are no other significant differences in performance in any other age group. It should be noted here that there is a wide spread in the age of pupils in Primary VII. This range is not always present in every classroom and there is a growing trend toward a lessening of the range through a standardization of age of entry to Primary I. There are observable differences in the average age of pupils in different regions, and even in different schools within a region. The mean age of pupils in Kampala is lower than the mean age for pupils in rural areas.

Some of the other variables which were evaluated indicate the type of controls which need to be considered in setting up experimental programmes. There is a significant indication that many of the differences which appear significant are related to the urban-rural distribution of the pupils. Table 3.10 shows this distribution for the high and low scorers. The chi-square is 6.16, significant at the 1 per cent level. In order to test this difference further we divided the entire group according to location. The mean score of the Kampala group was 16.52 ($t=5.13$); the mean score of the rural group was 15.94. This means that going to school in Kampala greatly increases an individual's chance of success in English.

TABLE 3.10: *Kampala-rural distribution of high and low scorers.*

	Kampala	Rural
High scorers	45	158
Low scorers	26	177

The Kampala schools in our sample had a much higher proportion of teachers in Primary VII who held Grade III Ministry Certificates (i.e. were better qualified). In order to determine whether the crucial factor in the success of the pupils in Kampala was the influence of the Grade III teachers, the scores were analysed for only the pupils who had a Grade III teacher in Primary VII and this group was divided into two groups—Kampala and rural. The mean score for the Kampala group was 16.84, higher than for the Kampala group as a whole and significantly higher than for the rural group whose mean score was 16.13. Having a Grade III teacher improves one's chances for success, but does not change the Kampala-rural difference.

Since the Kampala-rural difference was the most significant of all the statistical findings, a multiple and partial regression analysis of the data was performed on the entire group to determine the strength of the relationship of this factor and all of the others which were examined. The following nine variables were evaluated against individual scores in reading: (1) whether the child's first language was the same as that used in school in Primary I; (2) whether the child went to a school where English was the medium of instruction in Primary I; (3) whether the father spoke English; (4) whether the mother spoke English; (5) whether English was spoken at home; (6) when English was begun as a subject; (7) mobility of the pupil; (8) location and (9) aspirations. The multiple correlation coefficient for these variables was very low $(R=.14)$ accounting for only 2 per cent of the variance in the scores.

Even though there are individual variables which appear significant through chi-square analysis or comparison of mean scores, the multiple regression analysis indicates that the value of any one, or combination of these variables, is not very great for predicting an individual's success in reading English.

One important question remains unanswered. We do not know the effect of the English medium approach (teaching all subjects in English) from Primary I in a rural setting. None of the rural schools had been using English as the medium of instruction in Primary I

135

when the present Primary VII class which was tested had started school. This is a question which should be investigated.

Differences between Schools

The differences in scores from school to school indicate the possibility that achievement in English is dependent on certain factors within the schools themselves. In order to examine some of these factors, the six schools which scored highest on the reading test and the six schools which scored lowest (20 per cent of the total number of schools) were selected for further study. All six schools which scored low in reading were also low on the Primary English paper. Of the six top schools, all but one were above the mean on the same paper.

The first factor to be examined was the type of training which the teachers in the different schools had been given, as expressed in the Grade Ministry Certificate which they held. There was no difference in the number of Grade II teachers in the schools which were high and the schools which were low. There was a difference in the number of Grade I and Grade III teachers in the schools which were high and the schools which were low. The actual number is shown in Table 3.11. There are a larger number of better trained teachers (Grade III) in the schools which score high than in the schools which score low (chi-square = 3.69; p < 5). The positive effect of a better trained teacher was also noted in the analysis of the data for individual pupils.

TABLE 3.11: *Number of teachers holding Grade I and Grade III Certificates.*

	Grade I	Grade III
High schools	6	11
Low schools	11	5

Another area of expected difference among the teachers was in the years of teaching experience, independent of the type of training. New teachers, whatever their Grade Ministry Certificate, were not considered to be as effective as teachers who have had several years of teaching experience according to headmasters, District Education Officers, and people in the Inspectorate Division of the Ministry of Education. However, as the following table shows, none of these differences is great enough to be statistically significant.

TABLE 3.12:   *Number of years of teaching experience.*

	0–5	6–10	11–15	16–20	20+
Low schools . .	15	4	7	2	5
High schools . .	10	7	5	3	4

(Note: The total number of teachers is less than the full number to be expected in twelve schools. This is because not all the teachers in either group filled in the questionnaire.)

Although there was no significant difference in years of experience, when the data are examined in terms of the number of years teaching in a particular school (i.e. the mobility of the teachers) then there is a difference between the schools which score high and those which score low. In the schools which scored low there are more teachers who have been in that particular school for two years or less indicating that there may be a greater turnover of teachers in the low-scoring schools which causes a degree of instability in the staff as a whole and permits less continuity of the programme from year to year. The table below shows these figures. Chi-square corrected for continuity = 6.9; significant at the 2 per cent level. The stability of the staff appears to be a factor which affects the performance of the school as a whole.

TABLE 3.13:   *Years of teaching in the present schools.*

	Less than 2 years	More than 2 years
Low schools	23	10
High schools	11	19

One further difference between the teachers in the schools which scored high and those which scored low is in the number of teachers who report having had a special course in the teaching of English. These numbers are shown in Table 3.14. More of the teachers in the schools which scored high have had a special course in teaching English and this difference is again statistically significant (chi square = 4.06; $p < .05$).

TABLE 3.14:   *Number of teachers having a special course in English.*

	Yes	No
Low schools	10	22
High schools	17	13

The questionnaires revealed a great variety of in-service courses in the teaching of English, from intensive one-day workshops to three-week courses at special centres around the country. But no one type of in-service training appeared to be substantially better than all others. Follow-up interviews with teachers and tutors at the training colleges, as well as Ministry officials, indicated that the greatest benefit derived from the in-service training was related more to recognition of the teachers who participated in the programmes than to the actual content of such programmes.

Three factors relating to teacher training and experience appear to affect the performance of children on the reading test. These factors —Grade Ministry Certificate (I and III), mobility, and training in English—are relatively independent variables. The fact that a teacher holds a Grade I or Grade III Certificate will not indicate either the number of years the teacher has been in the present school, nor whether he has had a course in teaching English. The same is true of all other groupings. It does seem possible, however, that there is an additive effect of all of these variables. In other words, weakness in any one of these three might be compensated for by additional strength in one or both of the other variables.

In order to test this assumption further, the schools were divided into groups which corresponded roughly to the districts in which the schools were located. Two schools in Bukedi District were grouped with the Teso District schools since they are located in an Ateso speaking area of Bukedi District which is contiguous with Teso District. The mean score for the schools in the district was calculated and the totals on all of the teachers in each of the districts on the three variables were calculated. A multiple regression analysis of the data for nine districts with more than four schools in each district indicates that the three factors have a significant effect on school performance ($R = .91$) and in fact account for 83 per cent of the variance between schools. The same test on thirteen districts, including four with only two or three schools in each district, is considerably lower ($R = .51$). The same multiple regression analysis by schools rather than by districts yields an R of .41.

It would appear that all of these factors relating to the teachers' training and posting do affect the overall performance of children in English reading. Perhaps the importance of the teacher is already well enough known, but the statistical evidence adds considerable force to the argument for better training of teachers, both pre-service and in-service, and points to the need for great stability of staff.

Scores in English and Vernacular Languages Compared

The mean score for the group as a whole, excluding native speakers of English, Swahili, Gujerati, Hindi, or any non-Ugandan language, was 3.89 on the vernacular passage and 3.85 on the English passage (1,231 cases). The overall ability to read English is equal to the ability to read one of the six vernacular languages.

The mean score for the pupils who spoke one of the six vernacular languages as a first language was 4.03 on the vernacular passage and 3.84 on the passage in English, indicating a slight superiority in the vernacular passage (907 cases).

The mean score for pupils who spoke a vernacular language related to the official vernacular but not identical was 3.76 on the passage in the related vernacular and 4.08 on the passage in English, a slight superiority in English (278 cases)

The mean score for pupils who spoke a vernacular language not related to the language of the test was 2.11 in the vernacular passage and 4.00 in English, indicating a distinct superiority in English (46 cases).

Findings

The major findings of this study indicate that the areas of greatest importance in considering the effectiveness of the present instructional programme in teaching English to Ugandan children lie more in environmental factors than in individual sociolinguistic differences between pupils. The fact that urban children generally do better than their rural counterparts has been observed in many countries of the world. The urban child is exposed to a wider variety of external forces which both stimulate and reinforce school learning. He has a wider variety of books and other reading material at his disposal, more opportunity to use what he has learned at school in his everyday life, and the opportunity to observe and participate in a wider range of activities. In the case of English, the urban child is more likely to hear the language spoken around him in shops, on television, in the movies and among his peers than the rural child. Generally, the parents of children in an urban area are more highly educated than those in a rural community. All of these factors, plus others, are offered as plausible reasons for urban-rural differences. But these remarks must be tempered with a cautionary note. Although the mean score of the Kampala group is higher than the rural group *as a whole*, there are several districts that score as high or higher than the Kampala sample, e.g. Kigezi, 16.61 and Teso, 17.15.

There are undoubtedly social and cultural differences between the people who live in the different districts which account for some of the variation between the districts. However, a significant amount of the variation can be understood in terms of several factors related to teacher performance. The effectiveness of the instructional programme in English is determined in large measure by the teachers—their training and experience.

The Grade III teachers are more effective than the Grade I teachers. In-service training is important in improving teacher performance. Effectiveness increases with the time spent in a particular school. Perhaps one of the most significant things to be considered is that all of these aspects of teacher behaviour can be externally altered, a fact which has great significance in programme improvement.

None of the factors relating to the individual was seen to be of great importance in predicting success in learning to read English.

CONCLUSIONS

The results of this study offer statistical support to a readily observable fact: the success of the present policy to teach English in Uganda is dependent on the availability of teachers who can implement that policy.

There is great emphasis in Uganda at present on developing new material for the teaching of English. The problem with this approach is that it does nothing to insure any greater success than what is presently being achieved. New materials in the hands of the same teachers will not necessarily improve the language teaching.

The same is true of the emphasis on beginning English instruction as early as possible. Two extra years of poor teaching is not a guarantee of success. It is possible that the best approach would be to delay the introduction of English until the third year of primary school, using the Grade I teachers in the first two primary classes where English is not used at all. This means that teachers who have been better trained can begin the English language teaching in Primary III. The results of this study indicate that there are no significant differences between the groups who started English in

140

Primary I, II or III. English in Primary I might be a future goal of the Uganda Government, but in the absence of trained teachers it is doubtful whether two extra years of poor instruction contribute much to the level of performance in English.

The question of the Grade III teachers needs careful consideration. They are being trained in increasing numbers. The procedure at present is to post these teachers to Primary VII although a few are posted to Primary I. Their influence on the level of performance in English is observed in the fact that children in Primary VII who had a Grade III teacher did score higher than those who did not. The additional training and a higher standard of English in this group of teachers offer a measurable advantage to the pupils. What is not known is whether this is the most effective means of utilizing these teachers. Further research is needed on this point.

A practical consideration of the present programme is the issue of English medium instruction. The policy of the Ministry of Education is designed to produce a level of competence in the use of English which will enable all teaching to be done in English by the sixth year of school. Although no attempt was made to establish grade level norms for the reading test, it was obvious that the results of the test indicated a lower level of competence than that which is necessary for most pupils to read the subject-matter texts currently in use, despite the fact that a small percentage who reach secondary school are able to.

Despite enormous logistic problems in implementing the present language policy, the question is no longer one of whether to teach English, but *when* and *how* to do it most effectively. This study cannot even begin to answer such questions, but the results do point to the direction which future research must take in order to assure the success of the English language policy.

The need for research in the field of second-language teaching is virtually unlimited. Several studies which are suggested by the present research deal with the posting of teachers in order to utilize their skills in the most beneficial way.

At present there are 1,328 Grade III teachers in Uganda. There are 2,648 primary schools. Where should these teachers be posted to make maximal use of their training? Future plans include training all teachers to the level of the present Grade III teachers. It would be an advantage to know how the skills of these people can be used best as more of them are trained, but before all teachers reach this level of training. Some questions that need to be considered are: (1) whether posting Grade III teachers to Primary I results in the greatest gain for the school as a whole or to the pupils individually; (2) whether a Grade III teacher has the greatest impact in Primary VII; or (3) whether a Grade III teacher could serve best by teaching English in all classes from Primary I through Primary VII. And this list is certainly not exhaustive.

There are still more than 8,000 Grade I and unqualified teachers in Uganda. It will take a considerable time before better trained teachers will be available to replace them. In the interim, what is the best way to utilize this large body of teachers? How can their skills be strengthened? What is the most effective type of in-service training? Can team teaching be used as one method of strengthening the instructional programme?

The question of subject-matter mastery is a very real problem in a country where primary education is terminal education for the vast majority of pupils. Are the goals of education being met in a situation where a second language is used as a medium of instruction? Is there a difference between using English or an African language for this purpose? There is an opportunity to do cross-cultural research on this question in the next few years. Tanzania has adopted a policy of using Swahili as the sole medium of instruction in primary school and teaching English as a subject. Uganda is moving in the opposite direction and already has several schools where English is the sole medium of instruction from Primary I. Pupils in the two countries could be tested both on subject-matter mastery and on English language competence to determine the basic differences between the two approaches.

One final area of research should also be mentioned although it is beyond the scope of this study, and that is the issue of materials used in teaching English in the primary schools. Carefully controlled experimental tests are needed to determine the best approach for Ugandan children, and this leads ultimately to the need for research in how children learn.

There is a fertile field for study in Uganda. The success of any policy is dependent on understanding how to make it work.

The Teaching of the Vernacular Languages in Uganda

Livingstone Walusimbi

LANGUAGE POLICY

The Ministry of Education officially recognizes six language groups, namely Ateso/Akarimojong, Luganda, Lugbara, Lwo, Runyankore/Rukiga and Runyoro/Rutooro. These languages are expected to be taught at all levels of school education and teacher training colleges. But at the moment Luganda is the only vernacular taught up to School Certificate level. The rest are taught in primary schools and teacher training colleges only.

Ateso is the official language in Teso. But Kumam, a dialect of Lwo, is used unofficially as a medium of instruction in Kaberamaido County. Like many other languages or dialects in the Eastern region, Kumam is not written and therefore Ateso is used for writing purposes.

Although Ateso and Akarimojong are recognized officially as one language group, in practice it does not work. Books written in Ateso are not accepted wholly in Karamoja and yet there are hardly any written materials in Akarimojong suitable for school children.

Luganda is taught in all primary schools in Buganda (except in some urban schools) and it is the official medium of instruction in the lower primary in Busoga, Bugisu, Bukedi and Sebei, and it is expected to be taught as a subject in those areas. But since independence, the teaching of this language has deteriorated tremendously in all districts except Buganda. In practice all schools in those areas use their local languages and dialects, and in a few schools Luganda is taught as a subject. Some of these languages or dialects have no standard orthography and others are not written at all. Therefore pupils' written work is eventually done in Luganda. What a confusion to the children!

West Nile District in the North-West of Uganda, like some parts in the Eastern region, consists of several small tribes namely Madi,

Kakwa, Alur and Lugbara. These tribes are not linguistically related. Yet Lugbara is recognized as the official language in the area. This is a real problem because the rest of the tribes are very resentful toward the teaching of Lugbara in their schools. In fact in many schools they do not teach it—local languages are taught instead in spite of having no written materials for reading.

The Lwo group which is a composite of Acholi, Lango, Kumam, Alur, Dhopadhola and Jonam, is the most confused group. Acholi is the recognized form of Lwo. The rest are merely dialects of Acholi. But none of the native speakers of these dialects accept Acholi. Therefore at present there is no standard orthography acceptable to all Lwo speakers. Books written in Acholi are not welcomed in Lango, Kumam and other areas where Lwo is used. Each area uses its local dialect in teaching though no written literature is available except a few books in Lango.

Runyankore/Rukiga is wholly accepted as one form of language in Ankole and Kigezi and it is taught without any difficulty. All books are written in one form of language using the same orthography.

Runyoro/Rutooro, like Runyankore/Rukiga, is accepted by Banyoro and Batooro as one language for teaching and other purposes. Historically Banyoro and Batooro were one tribe and one can firmly say that Rutooro is a mere dialect of Runyoro.

SYLLABUS

The present vernacular syllabus is on the right lines, but it is too brief and vague to enable the majority of untrained language teachers to do their work properly. In fact many primary teachers find it difficult to follow. A more detailed and clear syllabus is urgently required now as there are not sufficient nor suitable books in all languages to assist teachers to teach effectively.

TIME ALLOCATION

In most primary schools throughout the country, vernacular language instruction is given the recommended time allocation on the timetable, i.e. an average of ten 30-minute periods per week in lower primary and three 40-minute periods in upper primary.

144

But the vernacular is not taught in many schools, particularly in the Northern and Eastern regions where, as mentioned in the foregoing paragraphs, there is a lot of disagreement about the official languages. In Buganda and Western region there are few problems.

TEACHING

It is accepted by the Ministry of Education and the National Institute of Education that vernacular is the worst taught subject in primary schools and teacher training colleges. In schools where this subject is taught, lessons consist of nothing but story telling, reading aloud, riddles and formal grammar, and are badly taught generally. Vernacular is regarded by both teachers and pupils as a pass-time lesson. Neither teachers nor pupils take this subject as seriously as they take other subjects. As a matter of fact, many teachers state categorically that children are not interested in their languages, they are more interested in English. (This is a sad allegation caused by lack of adequate knowledge of the subject matter and proper methods of language teaching.)

The problem of vernacular teaching in Uganda is affected by many factors namely:

(1) Lack of language teachers adequately trained to carry out their responsibilities. Many of our teachers are trained as English teachers specifically and not as language teachers in general. When they teach any other language they hardly think of employing or adapting methods used in teaching English. The primary school syllabus states on language policy that every attempt should be made to combine and relate the teaching of English and the vernacular— as language teaching. But teachers are not given an opportunity to explore the possibility of interrelating the methods of language teaching. At teacher training colleges where vernacular is taught, there are usually two tutors dealing with language teaching methods. One is confined to English and another to vernacular methods and they rarely meet to discuss their teaching methods or other problems.

(2) Lack of suitable and sufficient number of books for teachers and pupils. In most languages, books used are out of date and some are not suitable for school children. In fact, in some areas books written for the adult literacy campaign are now finding their way into

the classrooms. This, by itself, is not a bad thing as it is increasing reading material. But it appears to be encouraging the use of unofficial languages and dialects in the education system, which is contrary to the language policy.

Language courses are desperately needed. Two years ago a Uganda Language Series was started, sponsored by Longmans of Uganda. The first book, in Runyoro/Rutooro, will soon be available. Other language editions will follow at regular intervals. Teacher's handbooks and references are also badly needed. At present there is no single handbook for teachers in any language except Luganda. Fortunately the Vernacular Panel is now in the process of compiling a teacher's handbook written in English. We hope when it is completed it will be of great help to teachers.

(3) Uncertainty of the future of the vernacular languages makes many people, including teachers, inspectors of schools, education officers and parents, less interested in the subject. And although the language policy states, 'it is essential that the prime importance of the teaching of the vernacular languages be recognised', there appears to be no drive to enforce this. Vernacular is regarded as an optional subject and very few inspectors care to inspect how it is taught so that they may assist or advise the teachers concerned. This attitude is regrettable because it is now accepted on authority that vernacular plays a vital role in education. To quote the resolution passed in Rome in 1930 by the International Institute of African Languages and Culture, concerning the use of the vernacular in education:

It is a universally acknowledged principle in modern education that a child should receive instruction both in and through his mother tongue, and this privilege should not be withheld from the African child. The child should learn to respect the mental heritage of his own people, and the natural and necessary expression of this heritage is the language. Neglect of the vernacular involves the danger of crippling and destroying the pupil's productive powers by forcing him to express himself in a language foreign both to himself and to the genius of his race.

Mr. Gordon Watt-Wyness, the former Senior Inspector of Schools in charge of English language in primary schools in Uganda, had a strong feeling that vernacular and English should always receive equal attention and that there must be a cooperative and coordinated study of English and home language teaching. He wrote to me, as chairman of the Vernacular Subject Panel, saying,

146

As you know, however, I have long felt that we could possibly improve both vernacular and English by trying to develop some consultation. I don't myself accept that English is necessarily detrimental. It often is because of misguided attitude of teachers, but it needn't be. In particular I feel strongly that *Permanent Literacy* must be a concern of both of us, and that perhaps the greatest achievement in primary education would be if we could achieve that Permanent Literacy in both languages. *Good habits* of reading in both languages could be mutually beneficial.

Again in his remarkable report on English medium he wrote:

It is probable (to my mind anyway) that for some years to come we shall want, here in Uganda, a *sensible balance* between the English language and the home language, each playing its part. We cannot afford to waste our pitifully few resources by trying to go in different directions at once.

(4) The over-stress of the importance of the English language also affects the teaching of the vernacular languages in primary schools and teacher training colleges. It is true English plays a very important role in education in Uganda. It is the vehicle of all our learning at a higher level in education. Teachers as well as parents believe that English is the only means which will enable their children to pass the Primary Leaving Examination, to enter secondary schools or any other post-primary institutions and eventually to secure good jobs. English, to many people, means life. But our education system is planned in such a way that at present very few people profit by it. The majority of children who do not succeed in gaining places in secondary schools or any other institution of higher learning or training are always at a disadvantage. Their knowledge of English is very limited and their vernacular is also inadequate. Yet these are the majority of the citizens of Uganda—citizens with 'ill-conceived and inadequate language instruction'. They fit in neither educated society nor in the uneducated one because they cannot express themselves fully in either language. Communication becomes a problem. All this is caused by too much emphasis put on English and neglect of the home languages at the primary level.

(5) Vernacular is not recognized as an examination subject. Therefore teachers as well as pupils do not take it seriously and whenever there is need for more time to cover an English or Mathematics syllabus, periods for vernacular are cut down or the whole time allocated to the subject is taken over.

Teachers with some training in infant methods are today working very hard to improve the standard of oral work. Children are encouraged to speak freely but usefully in the classroom. A lot of oral work is usually given to children. But this good work started by the infant teachers is very often hampered by the teachers in the upper classes. Teachers in Primary III onwards take very little trouble to improve pupils' speech and vocabulary. Oral lessons are seldom organized and sometimes do not have proper aims. Story telling and riddles are the most popular topics taught during oral lessons.

Reading is receiving due attention particularly in the lower classes, but it is not taught well enough to achieve permanent literacy. In the upper classes reading is mainly done aloud round the class or in groups, and teachers usually do not bother to prepare their reading lessons. Intensive reading is not practised. Extensive reading is difficult to put into practice due to lack of sufficient supplementary readers.

Writing also is stressed in the infant classes, but it is the mechanical process which is emphasized more. Teachers forget that writing is a tool for language expression. Children are not encouraged to write creatively or to use writing for practical purposes. All children in a class are usually made to copy the same type of writing and more time is spent on practising handwriting which sometimes is not meaningful. Worse still, good handwriting is only stressed during writing lessons. Pupils are rarely encouraged to write legibly when doing other lessons.

Spelling in all languages is still a problem. Lwo, Lugbara and Ateso/Akarimojong have no standard orthographies acceptable to all speakers of these languages and therefore spelling conventions are very difficult to enforce. For Luganda, Runyoro/Rutooro and Runyankore/Rukiga, the standard orthographies which were originally set up in 1947 are now accepted by all speakers of these languages. But, of course, many people including teachers themselves still find spelling quite difficult to master. Children frequently make spelling mistakes and are not helped to improve because teachers themselves are not any better than they are.

Misuse of proverbs and idiomatic expressions is another common mistake made by pupils both in writing and speaking. Again because most teachers' knowledge of the language is not sound enough, pupils' mistakes are often not corrected. Nowadays there is a sort of language spoken by educated people. This form of language is neither English nor vernacular. It is a mixture of the two. The roots of the words are English but the prefixes and suffixes are vernacular e.g. **oku-post-inga** (to post). This is a very popular way of speaking in all languages today, and is now cropping up in schools. Pupils are mixing up vernacular and English in writing and in speech. Besides mixing up vernacular and English words, English ideas and expressions are also literally used quite often in vernacular and a listener or reader may not follow unless he has some knowledge of English.

Vernacular teaching in teacher training colleges is even worse than in primary schools. Colleges lack interested and able tutors who can teach vernacular. Some colleges are not interested in teaching these languages in spite of the fact that their students, after completing their training, are expected to teach a vernacular language or use it as the medium of instruction. Such colleges take vernacular as an optional subject and in some cases it is dropped from the college curriculum. A few colleges do not encourage their students to practise their knowledge of vernacular. Students are deprived of their right to speak their languages at the college campus except during vernacular lessons, if it is taught at all. In one college students are not even allowed, by college regulations, to read any vernacular book except during language lessons and lunch hours. When a student is found reading such books outside that time, he is punished.

It must be appreciated, however, that some colleges are still failing, with all effort, to get able tutors to teach vernacular effectively. A few other colleges in Eastern and Northern regions have students of various language groups. In such colleges it is rather difficult to cater for all the official languages.

Lack of adequate and suitable reading materials also makes vernacular teaching in colleges very difficult. In many cases, books recommended for use in primary schools are the same used in colleges for professional and academic purposes. This is a difficult problem and there seems to be no immediate remedy. The Vernacular Panel is doing all it can to advise colleges to encourage their students to produce materials which can be compiled and printed. We hope, if this is done, it will help in minimizing the shortage of supplementary readers both in schools and colleges. In addition, the Panel is planning, with the approval and sponsorship of the Ministry of Education and the National Institute of Education, Makerere University College, to organize a workshop for tutors which would make college tutors themselves produce suitable reading materials for their students. The Panel has also submitted a suggestion to the

Professional Board of the National Institute of Education asking it to approach the Ministry of Education about releasing some teachers and civil servants for a length of time to enable them to write language books.

If the Uganda languages are to be taught effectively throughout the country, a lot of things ought to receive careful attention. First the language policy requires full implementation. All schools should be made to teach the official language of the area and everything possible should be done to interest teachers in the subject and encourage them to regard vernacular as an important subject in the curriculum. Where it is practically impossible to use the official vernacular as a medium of instruction in the first year, it should be taught as a subject and be introduced as a medium in the second year. English medium schools also should not be exempted from teaching the official vernaculars used in the areas where they are situated, that is, a school in Soroti town or Kampala city should teach Ateso or Luganda respectively, as a subject.

Secondly, in order to enforce the language policy there must be enough teachers trained in language teaching. It is therefore necessary to put more emphasis on teacher training colleges in this respect. All colleges without any exception should teach vernacular and should give it equal importance to any other language taught there. Vernacular tutors also should receive opportunities to train in language teaching both at home and abroad. The Institute of Education's Associateship courses which are intended for teacher trainers, should include vernacular teaching.

In order to make teachers and children regard vernacular as an important subject and to encourage them to love it, the Primary Leaving Examination should include a vernacular paper, and the certificate awarded to successful candidates should consist of all school subjects, vernacular included. Admission to secondary schools should not be based entirely on the candidate's performance in English and Mathematics. All subjects done at primary level are very useful and important in the children's individual lives and they should be considered when admitting pupils to secondary and other post-primary institutions.

To enable teachers to teach vernacular to a certain degree of perfection and with interest and to cause pupils to love their languages, there must be good books in sufficient numbers. The Government should therefore assist authors and potential writers financially

150

or otherwise to produce as many books as possible. Where it is necessary, able teachers and Government civil servants should be released for a given time to write required books. The Uganda Education Commission Report published in 1963 also recommends the release of teaching or Ministry staff to write necessary books for schools. But the report warns:

It must be borne in mind that commercial publishers will not undertake the printing of books in any language unless the potential sales warrant the risk, and we could consider it unwise for the Central Government to finance publication of books in areas where the potential sales were so small as to make it impossible for them to cover the costs.

151

L

Appendix

THE READING TEST

Elephants

The elephant is the only animal in the world with a trunk. It uses its trunk in many ways. It pulls leaves off trees with its trunk and then puts them into its mouth. It can even use its trunk to pull up trees when it wants to make a path through the jungle. It also uses its trunk to get water. The trunk can hold a lot of water, as an elephant needs to drink more than three hundred pints of water every day.

When an elephant is angry, its tusks can be very dangerous. The tusks of an elephant are really its front teeth. People pay a lot of money for the ivory of an elephant's tusks. In Africa men have hunted elephants for their tusks. The ivory from the tusks is made into very beautiful things.

It has been easy for men to train elephants in Asia. They use elephants to carry heavy things for long distances.

Many people say that the kings of Siam used to give white elephants to people whom they did not like. These white elephants were sacred and they could not be made to work. They could not be killed or given away. A person who owned a white elephant had to pay a lot of money to keep it properly. After a certain time, he usually became very poor. Nowadays people often call a useless thing 'a white elephant'.

1. Elephants use their trunks to eat
   (a) animals
   (b) leaves
   (c) trees
   (d) ivory
2. An elephant's tusks are made of
   (a) bone
   (b) teeth
   (c) ivory
   (d) many beautiful things

3. In Africa men hunted elephants because
    (a) the tusks were valuable
    (b) elephants were very dangerous
    (c) hunting was interesting
    (d) elephants were very beautiful
4. Elephants are used to carry heavy things because
    (a) their tusks are useful
    (b) they are not dangerous
    (c) they are very strong
    (d) their trunks hold a lot of water
5. Siamese kings gave white elephants to people
    (a) as a sign of friendship
    (b) because people liked elephants
    (c) because elephants were useful
    (d) whom they did not like

New Hospitals

The opening at Iganga of the first of the new rural hospitals is a big event in the development of health services in this country. By building 23 such hospitals, spread throughout Uganda, the Government is not only increasing its medical facilities greatly, but it is implementing an important part of its policy to spread the benefits of modern development more evenly throughout the country. With 100 beds in each of these hospitals, there will be a large increase in the total of the medical facilities available, as well as a wider distribution of them. But expansion on this scale also brings its problems in finding the staff to man new hospitals and in meeting the cost of operating them.

It has involved an expansion in the training of medical assistants, nurses and midwives, as well as of doctors, and one effect of the large expansion of hospital services will be to increase the proportion of people in the service who have only a limited amount of practical experience. This will bring its own problems in the early years, but these can be overcome with the spirit of service and dedication to their tasks which the President has called for from all those who are involved.

Buildings alone do not make a hospital, and the success of the policy of providing new rural hospitals will depend on the services to be provided by their staffs. It is particularly important that their standards should be of the highest, because these institutions have a role to fill that it just as important as hospitals like Mulago which provides a greater range of specialized services.

1. The role of these rural hospitals is
    (a) to train medical assistants and doctors
    (b) to make Mulago more important
    (c) to provide general medical facilities
    (d) to lower the standard throughout the country

2. The new hospital at Iganga is
    (a) the only one of its kind which will be built
    (b) the first of 23 rural hospitals
    (c) the last of 23 rural hospitals
    (d) like Mulago

3. The problem of expansion is to get
    (a) enough beds
    (b) enough trained staff
    (c) the proper medicine
    (d) people to go to the hospital

4. Many people will have to be trained
    (a) to provide medical services
    (b) to build more hospitals
    (c) to work at Mulago hospital
    (d) to stop this expansion

5. The President has called on people
    (a) to become midwives
    (b) to see him if they have problems
    (c) to do only a limited amount of work
    (d) to dedicate themselves to their work

Yellow Fever

Yellow fever is a disease of warm lands, that is found mainly along the shores of the Atlantic Ocean. It was first noticed in the Americas, but may well have come from Africa and reached the New World with or soon after Columbus. Until about fifty years ago, yellow fever was still one of the most feared diseases in the United States, where many died in repeated outbreaks. An outbreak which was to lead to surprising developments was one that happened in Cuba during the Spanish-American War.

154

As a result, an army group under Major Walter Reed was sent there in June 1900 with orders 'to give special attention to questions concerning the cause and prevention of yellow fever'. In a daring group of experiments using human beings, Major Reed proved the truth of an idea advanced in 1881 by a Cuban doctor, that the city type of mosquito passed on the disease.

The successful result of these experiments gave birth to another and still more important idea: kill off the city type of mosquitoes and there will be no more yellow fever. Fortunately these mosquitoes are one of the easiest types to destroy. They are born in pools of quiet, warm water, within a short distance of people's homes.

A general came to Havana with orders from the United States Government to dry up these pools. He carried out his task so well that the mosquitoes disappeared. Yellow fever went with them, never to return to Havana. A few years later the same general successfully repeated this operation in Panama and in this way made possible the building of the Panama Canal. It all seemed so simple. End the mosquitoes; end the disease. Man even began to dream of getting rid of yellow fever from the world.

1. Yellow fever was a feared disease in the United States up to
    (a) 10 years ago
    (b) 25 years ago
    (c) 50 years ago
    (d) 100 years ago
2. The outbreak which stirred the interest of the Army was in
    (a) Cuba
    (b) Spain
    (c) Central America
    (d) the United States
3. The building of the Panama Canal was made possible by
    (a) the success of the Spanish-American War
    (b) the work of the United States Army
    (c) the killing of mosquitoes nearby
    (d) the development of special drugs
4. The first idea about ending the disease forever was to
    (a) remove people from yellow fever areas
    (b) have special spray poisons in every home
    (c) give everybody special drugs
    (d) kill all mosquitoes

5. Yellow fever is found mainly around
   (a) the Atlantic Ocean
   (b) the Pacific Ocean
   (c) the Indian Ocean
   (d) any ocean

Malaria

Malaria is the world's oldest recorded disease. It is referred to in old Chinese and Indian writings. It was one of the causes leading to the downfall of both the Greek and the Roman empires.

People recognized that there must be some connection between malaria and swamps, and some believed that insects living near swamps might be the carriers of the disease. The Romans dried the swamps and reduced the mosquito population. This was the best method used for the next fifteen centuries.

Not until 1632 did Europeans find a successful treatment for the disease. The Spanish discoverers of the New World learned from the Indians of Peru that the bark of one of the trees growing there often ended a patient's attack of malaria. In the nineteenth century French scientists found that quinine was the substance in the bark that cured malaria. The Dutch planted quinine trees in the East Indies and in time established an almost complete control of the medicine made from it. When the East Indies supply was cut off during the two world wars, two other drugs were developed which proved even more successful than quinine in curing attacks. Today most of the world uses these newer drugs.

The cure for malaria was found long before science learned the cause. During the last few years of the nineteenth century, however, the combined efforts of the scientists of several nations led to the discovery of the connection between swamps, mosquitoes and malaria. The first great step forward was made in 1879, when a young Scottish doctor working in China proved that another disease was spread by mosquitoes. This led to the discovery that mosquitoes were the carriers of malaria.

1. The connection between malaria and swamps
   (a) is just an old story
   (b) was known a very long time ago
   (c) has been proved not to be true
   (d) was discovered by the Chinese

2. We now know that the drug cure for malaria was found
    (a) before the cause
    (b) as a result of discovering the cause
    (c) after the cause
    (d) to be directly related to the cause
3. The cure for malaria was originally discovered
    (a) by a French scientist
    (b) in European laboratories
    (c) by Peruvian Indians
    (d) by Spanish explorers
4. The fight against malaria
    (a) has really just started in the last few years
    (b) has been going on for centuries
    (c) began in the 1800s
    (d) has been planned for the future
5. The discovery of the cause of malaria was
    (a) the result of a planned research programme
    (b) related to the discovery of poison sprays
    (c) made by a Chinese doctor
    (d) a result of another discovery

Agriculture

Uganda is still largely a country of farmers and more people are engaged in farming than in any other business. Agriculture is therefore Uganda's most important source of wealth. The crops grown in Uganda can be divided into two groups:
   (a) Food (or subsistence) crops such as matooke, finger millet, sweet potatoes, maize, groundnuts, sorghum cassava, etc.
   (b) Cash crops such as cotton, coffee, tea, tobacco, oil seeds, sugar, etc.
Subsistence crops provide food not only for the farmers who grow them, but for the nation as a whole. If there is any left over, it can usually be sold to another country. Cash crops provide the growers with the money they need for school fees, or for their clothing, cooking-pots, blankets and other things which they have to buy.

Crops depend on climate, that is rain and heat, so that some will grow well in one place and some in another. For this reason there

157

are farms run by the government at which new crops can be tried before farmers grow them.

The Department of Agriculture helps farmers to grow more and better crops in two ways:

(a) By advice. The field staff of the department visit farmers all over the country and help them to make the best use of their land. It is their job to give advice and encouragement to those farmers whose crops are spoiled by insects or disease, to those who plant their cotton at the wrong time or who fail to trim their coffee trees or weed their shambas.

(b) By research. By finding out more about what crops will grow, more about how to fight insects and plant diseases, and more about where crops will grow best.

1. In Uganda, the largest number of people are engaged in
   (a) business
   (b) government offices
   (c) farming
   (d) teaching

2. Crops grown in Uganda can be divided into
   (a) food and subsistence crops
   (b) cash crops and subsistence crops
   (c) matooke and sweet potatoes
   (d) cotton and coffee

3. The Department of Agriculture gives farmers advice about
   (a) how to make the best use of their land
   (b) how much coffee to drink
   (c) what crops they are allowed to plant
   (d) how to cook their food

4. Research helps farmers by
   (a) controlling the climate
   (b) finding out about plant diseases
   (c) finding out about human diseases
   (d) growing food for people

5. The climate is important in deciding
   (a) which plants grow best in a certain place
   (b) who should become a farmer
   (c) what to do about insects
   (d) how to weed your shamba

Ebibira

Mubyobugagga bya Uganda mwemubalirwa n'ebibira bya yo. Emiti girina emigaso mkumu. Abantu abasinga obungi bagyeyambisa ng'enku, okugizimbis'enju, n'okugikolamu ebintu byomunju, ng'emeeza entebe, n'ebirala. Naye ate era oluusi gyeyambisibwa ekitongole kya Post Office okusibako waya za Ssimu, n'ekitongole kya Uganda Electricity Board n'abomubirombe ekilembe. Egimu ku miti gya Uganda emigumu girina ebisaanyizo okutundibwa ebweru wa Uganda ne mungeri eyo negireetawo ekkubo eddala ery'okuyingiza ensimbi muggwanga.

Egya emigasogy'emiti ng'ogirese awo, emiti gikumira amazzi muttaka, era abantu bangi balowoza nti gireeta enjuba. Okusinziira kunsonga zino zonna ekisinga obukulu kwekulaba nti ebibira birabirirwa, era nut ng'emiti emito gitemeddwa wasaana wasimbibwewo emirala mukifo kyagyo. Singa kino tekikolebwa ekiseera kijja kutuuka wabe nga tewakyali miti gyakuzimbisa nju, kukola mu bintu, oba enku ezokufumbisa.

Mu Uganda mulimu ebibira nkumu ebikuumibwa, omutakirizibwa kutemwa miti ng'omuntu tafunye lukusa. Chief Conservator of Forests ne bakozi banne bebalabirira ebibira ebisinga obunenne kulwa gavumenti y'eggwanga. Ebibira ebisingawo obutono birabirirwa gavumenti ezebiundu.

Abalabe b'ebibira abakulu gwe muliro n'embuzi. Munsi ezimu omuliro gwonoona buli mwaka emiti egyandivuddemu obukadde n'obukedde bwa shillings. Embuzi zirya emiti emito, era mussaawa ntono butono ziyinza okwonoona omulimu ogututte emyezi.

1. Emiti gigasa abantu kulwa
    (a) masanyalage
    (b) kutwala bubaka
    (c) kuzimba nju
    (d) kuliisa mbuzi
2. Emiti gikumira amazzi
    (a) muttaka
    (b) mubirombe bye kilembe
    (c) mumayumba gabantu
    (d) mu Electricity Board
3. Emiti nga gitemeddwa
    (a) gisaana gyokebwe
    (b) gisaana giribwe embuzi

    (c) emirala gisaanye gisimbibwe mukifo kyagyo

    (d) kireeta enkuba

4. Mubibira ebikumibwa

    (a) tekikirizibwa kutema miti

    (b) tekikirizibwa kuba nambuzi

    (c) tekikirizibwa kukuma muliro

    (d) tekikirizibwa kutema miti awatali lukusa

5. Omuliro mulabe w'emiti kubanga

    (a) gwonona embuzi

    (b) gwokya amazzi gona ne gaggwawo

    (c) gukyusa embeera y'obudde

    (d) gwonoona emiti egyomuwendo

QUESTIONNAIRES

Pupil

1. We would like to know the names of all the schools you have attended up to the present. Please write in order the schools you attended and the number of years you attended. Start with your *first* primary school.

Name of School	Place (town)	Region	No. of Years

2. What is the first language you spoke? ....

3. What language did your teacher use when you were in Primary I?

....

4. When did you begin to learn English?

    [   ] at home

    [   ] in Primary I

    [   ] in Primary II

    [   ] in Primary III

    [   ] in Primary IV or after

5. Does your father speak English?

    [   ] YES   [   ] NO

6. Does your mother speak English?
     [   ]   YES   [   ]   NO
7. Do you ever speak English at home?
     [   ]   YES   [   ]   NO
8. What work does your father do? ......
9. What will you do when you finish Primary School if you do not get into Secondary School?
     [   ]   stay at home
     [   ]   go to Teacher Training College
     [   ]   go to Agriculture College
     [   ]   get a job in a shop
     [   ]   other ......
10. Age
11. Sex

Teacher

1. What class are you teaching this year? ......
2. What grade Ministry Certificate do you have? ......
3. Where did you receive your teacher training? ......
4. How many years have you been teaching? ......
5. How many years have you been teaching in *this* school? ......
6. What is your first language? ......
7. Did you ever have a course which prepared you specifically to teach English? ......
8. Where and when did you take this course? ......
   ......
9. Do you use any language other than English in the normal teaching day? ...... Which one? ......
10. What subjects are the most difficult for you to teach in English?
    ......
11. Where do you go for help when you are in doubt about a point of English grammar or usage? ......
    ......
12. Do you have any suggestions or comments about the problems of using English as a medium of instruction? ......
    ......
    ......
    ......

161

Headmaster

1. Name of school ....
2. County (saza) .... Gombolola .... Village ....
3. Foundation body ....
4. How many classes are there in the school? ....
5. What languages are spoken as a mother tongue by the pupils and how many speakers of each are there? ....
....
6. What vernacular is used in Primary I? ....
7. It is school policy to begin teaching English in Primary I, but sometimes this is not possible because there are no teachers who speak English or because there are no books or materials. In what class is English introduced as a subject here? ....
....
8. In what class do you begin to teach other subjects in English?
....
....
9. In what class is all teaching done in English? ....
10. How many teachers in your school are vernacular teachers?
....
11. Who teaches English to the pupils in the vernacular teacher's class? ....
....
12. Does the school have a radio? .... In what classes is it most used?
....
13. What do you consider your biggest problem in your school?
....
14. What help do you get from the District Education Officer or his assistants?
....

162

Bibliography

Brownell, John A., *Japan's Second Language*, National Council of Teachers of English, Illinois (1967).

Castle, Edgar B., *Growing Up in East Africa*, Oxford University Press, London (1966).

Fodor, I., *The Problems in the Classification of the African Languages*, Hungarian Academy of Sciences, Budapest (1966).

Gale, H. P., *Uganda and the Mill Hill Fathers*, Macmillan, London (1959).

Greenberg, J. H., *The Languages of Africa*, supplement to *International Journal of American Linguistics*, 29.1 (1963).

Guthrie, Malcolm, *The Classification of the Bantu Languages*, Oxford University Press, London (1948).

——, *Comparative Bantu*, Volume I, Gregg Press Ltd., Farnborough, Hants, England (1967).

Hindmarsh, Roland, 'Uganda' in Scanlon (ed.), *Church and State in Education*, Teachers College Press, Columbia University, New York (1966).

Ingham, Kenneth, *The Making of Modern Uganda*, George Allen and Unwin, London (1957).

Jacobs, Robert (ed.), *English Language Teaching in Nigeria*, A survey team report (1966).

Jones, Thomas Jesse, *Education in East Africa*, Phelps-Stokes Fund Study, Edinburgh House Press, London (1925).

Kiwanuka, P., 'Bilingualism in Education: The Role of the Vernacular Languages', *East Africa Journal*, 4.6 (1967).

Ladefoged, Peter, *A Phonetic Study of West African Languages*, Cambridge University Press, Cambridge (1964).

Ladefoged, Peter, 'The Measurement of Phonetic Similarity', *Statistical Methods in Linguistics*, 6 (1970).

Rice, Frank A. (ed.), *Study of the Role of Second Languages in Asia, Africa and Latin America*, Center for Applied Linguistics, Washington (1962).

Scanlon, David, *Education in Uganda*, U.S. Department of Health, Education and Welfare, Bulletin 32, Washington (1964).

Tucker, A. N. and M. A. Bryan, *The Non-Bantu Languages of North-Eastern Africa*, Oxford University Press, London (1956).

——— ———, *Linguistic Analysis: The Non-Bantu Languages of North-Eastern Africa*, Oxford University Press, London (1966).

Williams, Peter, *Aid in Uganda*, Overseas Development Institute Ltd., London (1966).

Zake, Hon. S. J. Luyimbazi, 'Educational Revolution in Uganda' in *The Challenge of Uganda's Second Five Year Development Plan*, Government Printer, Entebbe (1966).

Index

Printed by English Press, P.O. Box 30127, Nairobi
and published by Oxford University Press, P.O. Box 72532, Nairobi.